Leadership in Whole Language

Leadership in Whole Language

■

The Principal's Role

Bob Wortman
*Principal, Borton Primary Magnet School,
Tucson Unified School District*

and

Myna Matlin
*Principal, Warren Elementary School,
Tucson Unified School District*

Stenhouse Publishers
York, Maine

Stenhouse Publishers, 226 York Street, York, Maine 03909

Library of Congress Cataloging-in-Publication Data

Wortman, Bob, 1951–
    Leadership in whole language : the principal's role / Bob Wortman
and Myna Matlin.
        p.   cm.
    Includes bibliographical references and index.
    ISBN 1-57110-012-1 (alk. paper)
    1. Language experience approach in education—Arizona—Tucson—
Case studies.   2. School management and organization—Arizona—
Tucson—Case studies.   3. Elementary school principals—Arizona—
Tucson—Case studies.   I. Matlin, Myna.   II. Title.
    LB1576.W685   1995
372.6—dc20   95-16692
                                                                    CIP

Cover and interior design by Darci Mehall
Photographs by Joel Brown
Typeset by Octal Publishing

Manufactured in the United States of America on acid-free paper

99 98 97 96 95 8 7 6 5 4 3 2 1

Contents

Foreword

At a time when America is becoming increasingly concerned about the quality of its schools and the debate between phonics and whole language instruction has taken on religious overtones, Myna Matlin and Bob Wortman step into the breach to provide clear, compelling, no-nonsense answers to the questions of what might be done in this turbulent context.

I got to know Myna and Bob when I served as their superintendent in Tucson in the late 1980s. While each has a very different and distinctive style, they both serve as examples of what building leadership can do, demonstrating that good things happen in schools with good leaders.

Considering external influences, Warren and Borton are schools that should not be nearly as successful as they are. Yet these schools work for one basic reason—their principals have principles. Each principal provides calm, consistent leadership day after day. Myna and Bob show that principals do make a difference. They have crafted a book that tells you all you ever wanted to know about whole language and much more. In fact, *Leadership in Whole Language* is not merely a book about whole language, it is also a book about good school leadership. For those seeking to know much more about whole language and how to implement it, or for anyone concerned about what makes good building leadership, this book is a rare find.

Bob and Myna show that good principals in any school setting are organized and plan ahead. They know their school community, their teachers, and their students. They provide daily examples of dedicated, hard-working nuts and bolts leadership. At the same time, they show that strong leaders are human and understand how to have fun as they do their work. They also call for balance in leadership between the personal and professional life.

Leadership in Whole Language describes in detail what whole language is and isn't and what the whole language principal's supporting role can and should be. In my opinion, the most compelling chapter is Chapter Four, "Building a Community" because it explains that the essence of strong leadership in any context is the ability to build a community in and around the school.

Throughout the book there are many suggestions with concrete examples of the actions principals can take to improve learning and implement whole language instruction in their schools. Bob and Myna describe strategies for discipline, staff development and family interaction, concluding with a very powerful chapter on evaluation. The voices of students are interspersed throughout to make the point that whole language instruction is organic and grows from the soil of the learner. *Leadership in Whole Language* is a testament to the philosophy that Myna and Bob espouse: "leaders plant the seeds, nurture and live their visions."

Paul Houston

Preface

The Power of Leadership

by Yetta M. Goodman and Kenneth S. Goodman

Browsing through bookstores and libraries looking for whole language materials for teachers is an exciting experience. There is so much written about applying whole language principles in teaching social studies, math, science, literature circles, and inquiry into the development of democratic learning communities in the classroom. There are richly documented descriptions of the characteristics of whole language classrooms.

There is, however, much less written on the leadership of a whole language school from the point of view of the principal. It is therefore timely and appropriate to have a book that examines how whole language *principals* apply whole language *principles* in the organization and development of a democratic learning community within the whole school.

Bob Wortman and Myna Matlin are principals who *use what they know to inform what they do* as principals. They have each been involved in whole language theory, research, and teaching for many years. Myna Matlin's doctoral dissertation was a study of the literacy development of children in Bob's kindergarten. Bob's dissertation looked at the authenticity of writing events in his own classroom.

Bob and Myna each adapted their beliefs as they moved into principal roles. They have been successful in their administrative positions as attested to by the teachers with whom they work and the parents and children who are part of their school communities. No one is better suited to write a book on the role of the whole language principal as instructional leader in a whole language school than these two highly experienced, committed, and acclaimed professionals. People who have heard us speak know that we often refer to Bob and Myna (we use their first names because of our long and friendly relationship as colleagues) as examples of principals establishing whole language pedagogy in the whole school environment. They support whole language teachers in the organization of whole language curriculum, and they apply their knowledge of whole language principles in their professional relationships with all the members of their school community.

We often consult with them when we need to establish the links between whole language theory and practice. We respect their knowledge, their commitment, and their ability to show how theory and practice come together to establish a schoolwide learning community. We've seen their concepts of whole language leadership in action as we work with children and teachers at both Warren and Borton Elementary Schools.

Leadership in Whole Language raises and addresses a number of important issues that are significant to the establishment of whole language pedagogy. Bob and Myna see principals as instructional leaders, thus redefining the role of the principal. They exemplify this view in their own work as administrators. They attend and participate in professional development workshops with their teachers. They are often in classrooms as much to work with students as to support teachers. We have heard Bob read to a classroom of children. We have seen Myna use her expertise to help teachers better understand their students' reading and writing abilities. They are knowledgeable about curriculum and speak with gentle authority about the latest controversies concerning subject matter areas. At the same time, they appreciate and are aware of the strengths of their teachers. They encourage teachers to be leaders in their areas of expertise. They participate in professional organizations and conferences and expect the same of their teachers.

In this book they describe well how the principal can help create a safe and secure environment in which children enjoy coming to school and the staff and faculty can take the risks which innovative education requires. Their teachers believe they are valued for their unique perspectives. Neither Bob nor Myna make any effort to establish a single kind of effectiveness for others to emulate. Neither of them promote one teacher over the other. On the other hand, they expect change and growth from their teachers. The strength of a whole school community working in concert to establish schoolwide learning opportunities is what this book sets as the goal of the whole language principal.

All aspects of modern urban schooling are political in nature and the book does not shy away from controversy. Myna and Bob believe that to support innovative practices principals must value constructive change and support new ideas that promote quality education for their students. They see principals as advocates for teachers and learners to the decision makers and the public. They show how principals must be able to articulate what is happening in schools that benefit children and make the good things schools are doing more visible to parents and the general public. This book will help parents and the public understand what effective principals need to do and know. It will help other administrators see the value of whole language for their pupils and teachers.

Authenticity is a key word in whole language. It means that what happens to kids in school is rooted in the real world. Bob Wortman and Myna Matlin have written an authentic book for administrators. Everything in the book is rooted in their own experiences. They have done what they advocate principals doing in the real world of urban American schools—they have not attempted to clone themselves or create templates for other administrators. With this book, committed school administrators can reinvent themselves. And that will mean better schools for both teachers and learners.

Acknowledgments

Very special thanks to our patient and loving spouses, Jackie Wortman and Tony Poyner, for their support and technological know-how, which helped us with the writing process. Thanks to colleagues Liz Whitaker for her computer advice, Joel Brown for his photographs, and Dr. Kathy Short and Dr. Caroline Tompkins for their insightful editorial comments.

We are indebted to our mentors and friends Drs. Yetta and Ken Goodman, who introduced us to each other many years ago and continue to support us as learners. Finally, we thank the staff members, parents, and children of Borton and Warren, who continue to teach us so much.

Introduction

About Myna and Bob

In this book, we often write in one voice. Time and again you will see "we" and wonder about us. We do hold many similar views, especially about the teaching/learning process. We see ourselves as educational leaders and head teachers who are responsible for the educational practices taking place in our respective schools. We are responsible for the education of students, parents, members of the larger community, teachers, staff, and ourselves. We are always on the go.

Yet we are two very different people. Bob is outgoing and has a warm sense of humor. He is known for his puns and love of children's literature. When Bob forces himself to sit down at the computer, words flow. His first drafts read like a conversation. He speaks to principals and teachers around the country, writes for publication, maintains a busy family schedule that includes keeping track of two teenagers, and gardens when he can.

Myna is known for her organizational abilities and gets right down to business. She sometimes needs to be reminded to slow down and have fun. She is also a strong teacher advocate, writes for publication, and has a quiet sense of humor. Myna is introspective and would much prefer to write than to give presentations, although she gives her share of talks to educators. Her free hours are spent reading, telephoning her daughters and stepchildren, mailing off educational gifts to her grandchildren, and trying to relax.

Our elementary schools and student bodies differ too, even though we are principals in the same school district. The Tucson Unified School District (TUSD) is a large urban district (57,000 students) in the southwestern United States. Both our schools are small, and neither of us has an assistant principal.

Myna's school, Frances Warren Elementary, has approximately 420 students and is located in a suburban, almost rural, area of Tucson. It is in the open desert and is surrounded by small but striking volcanic mountains. It is a neighborhood school with an ethnically diverse student population—67 percent Hispanic, 27 percent Anglo, 3 percent Native American, 2 percent African American, and

1 percent Asian American. The socioeconomic status of the students also varies. Their families live in large single-family homes, mobile homes, and government-subsidized apartments. The average income is low; 70 percent of the students receive free or reduced meals at school.

Warren Elementary is a fairly typical TUSD school, although it was recently shown to be in the bottom quartile for receiving outside funding for educational programs. Warren obtains additional financial support through grants (State Dropout Prevention funds, a DeWitt Wallace–Reader's Digest grant, and Reading Is Fundamental (RIF) subsidies), perseverance, and begging.

Myna has been working with the TUSD Bilingual Education Department to establish a bilingual Spanish/English program at Warren. Classroom teachers are responsible for all areas of the curriculum. No specialists are available in the regular classrooms, but there is support from part-time Exceptional Education and Gifted and Talented Resource teachers. The Warren staff has worked extremely hard to integrate all students into mainstream classes.

Warren is a whole language school. The faculty has worked with Dr. Kathy Short over the past four years to build an effective literature-based literacy program and strong communication among the teachers, staff, and principal. The school has also hosted the University of Arizona Language, Reading, and Culture teacher preparation block program for three years in collaboration with Ken and Yetta Goodman. Myna and the faculty continually strive to improve the teaching and learning strategies at Warren.

Bob is at Elizabeth Borton Primary Magnet School, a whole language school of 260 students that has been under court-ordered desegregation for fifteen years. It is located in an inner-city neighborhood surrounded by industrial sites and businesses. The high rate of substance abuse and related crimes in the area is exacerbated by the presence of several rival street gangs.

The neighborhood population at Borton is primarily lower-income minority—approximately 65 percent Hispanic, 20 percent African American, 10 percent Native American and 5 percent Asian American. All kindergarten through third-grade students from the neighborhood attend Borton. Neighborhood fourth, fifth, and sixth graders are bused to another school in a predominantly European American neighborhood.

The court order requires the principal to maintain a 51 percent European American/49 percent minority balance in the school by busing students in from across the district. The majority of bused students enter as kindergartners, although a few first and second graders enter with "sibling status" to keep families together. There is a waiting list of about one hundred European American students for the twenty-five kindergarten openings each year. (Students must be on the waiting list before they are a year old to be assured placement.)

Borton receives additional desegregation funding but no Chapter I or other compensatory program support. The court order provides for smaller student/teacher ratios (20/1 in kindergarten and 25/1 in first through third grades), two specialists (a fine arts teacher responsible for music and art and a physical education teacher trained in creative movement and dance), and a full-time librarian. There are no specialists attached to most elementary sites in TUSD, and a school of Borton's size would normally qualify for only a half-time librarian.

The school has maintained a high profile in the community and has been the site for five major research studies that have documented the power of whole language classrooms in supporting student learning. It also serves as the University of Arizona's Professional Development Site for Ken and Yetta Goodman's Language, Reading, and Culture undergraduate teacher preparation block program in whole language. University faculty and Borton teachers collaborate to work with twenty-five education majors who take their teaching methods classes two days a week at Borton. These university students are engaged as apprentice teachers at Borton (and at Warren) for an additional day and a half a week.

Collaborating on this book has helped us clarify our understandings and beliefs about teaching and learning, strengthen our roles as educational leaders, and become better reflective practitioners. We want to share what we have learned from our whole language research and practice. In doing so, we invite you to engage in your own dialogue and reflect on your own whole language practices.

February 1995

Oct 19 1992

Dear Dr. Matlin.
Hi its Joey doing?
How are you
school is fun.
I wish we had have
school every day. Is the
Job fun? wat do you do for
fun? do you like too chravl?
I do. It is fun. I wish
i was a Prnsabl like
you. It looks fun.
I wish I cud stay
at school for aver. good bye
fram Joey

4

ONE

A Day in the Life of a Whole Language Principal

Principals' days have many similarities, yet vary with their personality, abilities, interests, the size of their school, and student and community makeup. We believe the educational philosophy and background of principals affect their daily schedules too, by determining where they focus their time and energy. Each day's schedule directly relates to their view of who principals are and what principals accomplish.

We see ourselves as learners and as educational leaders—teachers of staff, community members, parents, and students. We deliberately reflect and make decisions, schedule our days, and engage in daily interactions based on strongly held beliefs about how children and adults learn. We spend our time in shared decision making and interacting in classrooms and community settings. We demonstrate ideas and actions that promote natural learning for all.

We work at being consistent with school goals and our own whole language belief systems as we nurture and strengthen our community, lead in areas of curriculum and instruction, and make decisions affecting resources and building management. We believe it is important for us as whole language principals to interact with students, parents, and staff. Our schedules also provide ample opportunity for reflection and leave time to deal with management issues that continually arise at school.

We build in time at the beginning of the day to greet students and to be available to parents and staff. Whenever we can, we are also "out and about" after school and during peak traffic periods. We make it a point to walk through every classroom every day. We greet teachers, provide encouragement, ask students how they are getting along, and applaud positive behavior, especially with students who have had difficulties.

During those times when we are in the office, we make it a point to remain available and demonstrate our intense interest in learning. We are surrounded by the books we love, the journals we enjoy, and the paperwork we are tied to. We drop what we are doing to take advantage of the energy in those teachable moments when students come in to share their projects, read their stories, and discuss their favorite books.

It is the same when teachers, staff, or parents need our time, attention, and encouragement. It's easier to ask people to make appointments, but we are not willing to lose the enthusiasm of the moment.

In this chapter, we describe a "typical" school day in each of our lives in order to demonstrate how we as whole language *principals* put our whole language *principles* into action. We have left out district meetings, daily management concerns, and other crises with which principals deal: fielding complaints about broken heating or cooling systems (and getting them fixed) or calling a grandparent to pick up Rover after he has followed Angélica to school. These events, of course, are very real and intervene in our most precisely scheduled days.

Our Day Begins . . .

Obviously there are no regular days in the life of a principal. The following descriptions of a typical day, however, bring out the schedules and strategies we use to do our job. They also illustrate the importance we as whole language principals place on teaching and learning—whether of students, parents, staff, or ourselves.

Bob's Day

10:00 P.M. My best days at school begin the evening before as I organize my time for the next day. I take twenty to thirty minutes each evening to reflect on the following day, jot things down on self-stick notes, and put the notes into my appointment book.

I also respond to student letters I've received through the school postal system and write supportive notes to staff members acknowledging specific actions and special work.

6:50 A.M. I take ten minutes to look over my appointment book and my notes from the evening before. I add thoughts that have occurred during the night (at 3:00 A.M., say) and walk through my day in my head.

7:00 A.M. While driving my teenagers to school (I do have a life outside school!), I talk with them. I'm tempted to spend this time organizing my thoughts, but I remind myself to maintain the balance of personal/family/professional life. (Each Wednesday our site-based decision-making committee meets at 7:00 A.M. Needless to say, Wednesday mornings are hectic.)

7:30 A.M. Once I hit the building, my life is not my own. The teachers and most of the other staff members have already arrived. I answer questions, gather information, and touch base about kids and parents. I become resident head cheerleader. The degree to which I acknowledge, greet, and positively interact with staff members in the morning influences the social and emotional mood in the building for the rest of the day.

I pull together children's books that I am going to read to classes that day. It is part of my regular weekly schedule to read to all classes.

8:00 A.M. I meet with staff members during this last half hour before the school day gets under way. I hold conferences or staff meetings and deal with individual or interpersonal issues.

8:20 A.M. If there are substitute teachers, I make each one feel welcome and remind them to read "The Substitute" section of the teacher's plan books and to go over the regular room procedures with the students so everyone has clear expectations before the day begins.

8:30 A.M. When the bell rings, I greet the children entering the patio from the playground. This "grounds" me to the reason schools exist and allows me to give students a smile, a hug, or a kind word that lets them know I am happy they are at Borton.

The entire school meets each morning for the Pledge of Allegiance and announcements. Students gather with their teachers on the patio, and a different class each week leads us in singing a song. This focuses attention and channels energy quickly. Necessary announcements are made, and classes are dismissed to their classrooms. This daily ritual takes five to eight minutes and allows everyone to join together as a community.

9:00 A.M. I read in a different classroom each morning, barring a scheduled meeting or an emergency. I choose a book specifically for that class. The books usually deal with issues related to building a community, like name-calling or solving problems peacefully. This time lets me interact with each classroom in an instructional or problem-solving context rather than as a disciplinarian.

9:15 A.M. Just as teachers like uninterrupted instructional time each day, I prefer large blocks of time to be in classrooms. My daily walk-throughs demonstrate to students, parents, and staff that I care about instruction and about each student's being part of the school community.

Myna's Day

10:00 P.M. I head for bed after eating dinner, taking a walk with my husband, and spending thirty minutes to an hour finishing up projects from the day. I often sit at the computer at home and input a report or newsletter. It helps me finish one day and begin to look ahead to the next.

6:50 A.M. I have been in my car for at least five minutes on my way to school. During my forty-five-minute drive, I organize my thoughts for the day, deliberately practice breathing deeply, and listen to music.

7:00 A.M. I listen to the news on my car radio and keenly await the music to begin again so I can go back to my efforts to relax.

7:30 A.M. The office manager, most of the teaching staff, and I all arrive about the same time. It is important for me to be present as the school day begins. The day custodian has been in the building since 5:30 A.M. and several teachers have arrived at 7:00, but the rest of us begin our school day at 7:30.

On mornings when I have a lot on my mind and cannot sleep, I go to school early and enjoy a quiet time saying hello to the custodian and doing some paperwork.

Usually when I arrive at school someone is waiting for me and off I go!

In the morning my time is not my own. I am in the outer office as often as possible to say good morning and help establish a positive atmosphere for the day. I make a special effort to greet and smile at people who seem grumpy, but I rarely push for much response.

I also welcome substitute teachers and parents bringing their children through the office. I let substitutes know about any special events, such as fire drills or assemblies, and make sure they receive the substitute folder with school rules, plans, and schedules.

Sometimes I need to hold staff meetings or meet with someone during this time, although I prefer to leave the time unscheduled. I try to walk over to the cafeteria or out to the playground to say good morning to students eating breakfast and other early arrivals.

8:00 A.M. The bell rings. Whenever possible, I continue to greet students and parents as they enter the building from the playground. I am available to speak with parents who have questions or concerns. Occasionally I drive out to pick up a child who missed the bus, or I put journal articles I enjoyed reading into staff mail boxes.

8:20 A.M. I check in with the office staff and custodian, if I haven't already, to confirm priorities and schedules. They may want to discuss work-related issues, such as arranging fire drills or organizing work schedules to accomplish special projects. This encourages teamwork and facilitates problem solving.

8:30 A.M. I walk through the building, stopping at each classroom. When appropriate I say hello to the class. When everyone is engaged in quiet activities, I smile at individuals and sit down to observe or participate along with the teachers and students. This sometimes gives me a chance to read or write with a student the teacher and I have been discussing or to see what classroom groups are learning. Everyone knows this is my practice, and the normal routine rarely stops when I come into the room.

I carry a form (a modified version of one given to me by another principal) on a clipboard. I check off pertinent routines and practices I observe and write positive anecdotes about what is going on. Like Bob, I put a copy of these anecdotes in my evaluation file and give the teacher the original. I respond in writing or orally

Bob's Day (continued)

Although I try to visit every class every day, I usually take at least twenty minutes to focus on one class on a rotating basis. I carry a small pad on which I write anecdotes about interactions, activities, and feeling tone. Later, I copy these anecdotal records to put into my staff evaluation files and give the original to specific staff members.

There are many visitors to Borton, and one of my favorite activities is to escort them through the building. I am able to spotlight the strengths of each classroom and staff member. I have found there is great power in hearing the principal share "wonderful things" about staff members with others. It provides far more encouragement than face-to-face compliments.

10:30 A.M. I touch base in the office to return phone calls, keep specific appointments, and go through the morning's mail.

11:00 A.M. This is my time to meet with custodians, food service staff, and monitors as they prepare for the daily ritual of "lunch in the public school." It shows these vital employees that I value them. I also review plans for children who have lost their outside playtime privileges or hold problem-solving sessions.

11:30 A.M. There are two overlapping lunch periods of forty-five minutes each. The students only need half an hour, but the adults need forty-five minutes to feel they have had a break. I try to walk through the cafeteria and around the playground each day, to answer questions and get information. Sometimes I eat in the cafeteria with one or the other of the student lunch groups, and sometimes I eat with staff members in the lounge. A great deal of community-building happens during these informal times. I am generally on the run the entire time,

having what Hall and Hord (1987) call one-legged conferences.

There are child study team meetings during lunch each Monday. Teachers and auxiliary staff volunteer for a month at a time to meet with the team to help provide support for teachers who have questions about a student's behavior or academic progress. Either the Wednesday or Thursday lunch period is designated a working lunch meeting with staff members to deal with curricular concerns or plan schoolwide activities or inservices.

I also occasionally invite students to eat with me in my office to resolve conflicts, discuss important issues, or just have a comfortable time together.

12:45 P.M. Phew! Lunch is over! I meet with the monitors to collect any behavior notes that they wrote during lunch time. I copy these into the discipline log for future reference. I then meet with students who have had problems or make a note to meet with them the following day before lunch.

1:00 P.M. On my best days I take about fifteen minutes to sit peacefully at my desk listening to classical music and catch up on correspondence. I might write a letter to a student who has become an older brother or sister or has a family member in the hospital. Recognizing changes in the home is a powerful reminder to students and families that they are important to me. I always have at least one new children's book to read as my "treat" for the day. I save most professional reading for home (but I do keep current copies of *Young Children, Educational Leadership, Reading Teacher,* and *Language Arts* in my office bathroom).

I read to other classes after lunch or before dismissal. Sometimes I walk through classrooms; sometimes I stay put in one classroom for a while, especially if

Myna's Day (continued)

each time I am in a classroom, because I believe this helps teachers, staff, and students grow.

9:30 A.M. The official Uninterrupted Learning Time at Warren ends and students may leave classrooms to go to band, orchestra, or other out-of-classroom activities. I often head back to the office to check in and handle anything urgent. If things are relatively quiet, I go back out to classrooms to observe again. Sometimes I co-teach part of a class—over several days or intermittently—during a unit of study. Teachers are understanding when emergencies call me away in the middle of lessons, but my wonderful office staff often heads off problems or soothes feelings until I can deal with them.

10:45 A.M. I check in with the health office to get a report on problems that may have arisen there. Then I go into the office to see if there are important calls to return or students to see. I leave time to have students read to me or show me their accomplishments in writing or the content areas. I also see students who need extra "support" in managing their behavior—even whole language principals deal with discipline (see Chapter 5).

11:00 A.M. Our three overlapping lunch periods begin. I attempt to be in the cafeteria/multipurpose room as each group of classes enters. This gives me the opportunity to say hello to students informally and set the tone for a pleasant lunch. I am also available for a quick conference with any teacher who wants to chat.

11:15 A.M. I move between the cafeteria, playground, and office, interacting with students, staff, and visitors, attending to discipline issues, and on good days managing to eat my own lunch.

Every thirty-five minutes a bell rings. Students line up and teachers walk them into the building from the playground. I

like to be out on the playground as students go back to class to wish them a good afternoon's work.

12:40 P.M. The last lunch period is over! I call students who have had behavioral problems on the playground to my office and meet with them. When parents need to be contacted, I attempt to reach them by telephone immediately. Sometimes their children write them letters explaining the situation and requesting their written response.

1:00 P.M. I check in with the playground and cafeteria monitors and make a quick trip around the building. I briefly greet classes where there are substitutes and visit others on a rotating basis. I then go back to my office and with any luck will have thirty to forty minutes to attend to some management tasks and paperwork.

2:00 P.M. As the bell rings, I move out to the hallway to say good-bye to students and to be available to talk with parents. Some parents talk casually; others ask to make appointments. Students leave for home on buses, in cars, or on foot; some go to the multipurpose room to sign in for after-school recreation sponsored by the county.

When I go back to the office there is often someone, either a staff member or a parent, waiting to talk. There is a clip outside my office door where messages are left for me when I am in conference.

2:15 P.M. The staff and I use this time to meet and plan. On Mondays there are scheduled child study team meetings. Each quarter different teachers participate. Tuesdays alternate between staff meetings and a teacher study group that has been meeting for four years (Matlin and Short 1991). On afternoons when I am not away at district meetings I am available to meet with individual staff members, attend grade-level meetings, or plan with teachers.

Bob's Day (continued)

that wasn't possible in the morning, spending time with individual students and groups.

I make it a point to work on staff announcements, faculty agendas, and parent newsletters in classrooms whenever possible. I take along my disks and log on to a classroom computer, thus getting my work done and demonstrating the authentic uses I have for literacy in my job.

2:00 P.M. As parents begin to arrive to pick up their children, I am out in the hallway or patio. Parents are often reluctant to share concerns with the principal. This afternoon visibility is similar to my morning greeting routine, and I approach parents and continue to build trust. I say good-bye to students and let them know I look forward to their return the following day.

2:30 P.M. All students have boarded buses or are rushing to extended-day classes. This is when the staff begins to line up in the hallway to see me or to leave messages because I am meeting with parents or other staff members. Sometimes I am at district meetings.

The time after school is always hectic. The teachers go to the lounge to get a soft drink and in general get their second wind. It is not unusual for staff members at Borton to "drop in" to see me until five o'clock.

4:30 P.M. This is my most productive time to complete paperwork and tackle the daily mail. Most of the staff have left, so I can turn on some music and try to find the wood grain of my desk.

5:30 P.M. I usually leave for home, prepare for meetings (biweekly PTA executive board meetings, monthly PTA membership meetings, monthly School Community Partnership Committee meetings, monthly professional organization meetings), or drive my teenagers to basketball practices and games or musical theater rehearsals and performances.

6:00 P.M. On a good day I am home to start cooking dinner. There is some daylight to water the garden before I sit down to a quiet conversation with my wife and children.

10:00 P.M. I start preparing for tomorrow.

The Cycle Continues . . .

Myna's Day (continued)

3:30 P.M. This is the quietest part of the day. I have half an hour to catch up on business with the office manager before she leaves. It is an important time for me to communicate with her. Afterward I go through my mail, complete paperwork, and return telephone calls. I attempt to handle each piece of paper once and only once, as I have read all "good" administrators do, but I usually end up with at least three piles—done, to do, and to do again. Like Bob, I rarely clear my desk but always attempt to do so. Before leaving for the evening, I gather uncompleted tasks to take with me. On Thursdays I normally take home my file of items for the weekly staff newsletter.

5:00 P.M. I usually head for home, making an extreme effort to keep my mind on driving in the rush-hour traffic. On those rare afternoons when I leave the school at 4:00 or 4:30, I can almost count on finding a message from my regional assistant superintendent on my answering machine at home.

Some days I stay to prepare for meetings. If there is a late-evening meeting at school that other staff members will also attend, I may have an early dinner with some of them and use the time to build collegial relationships and talk "school."

6:00 P.M. Most days I am home discussing with my husband who is going to cook dinner or call for take-out. I often use him as a sounding board for my day because I value his "outsider" views.

8:30 P.M. I go to the computer and start thinking about tomorrow.

The Cycle Continues . . .

Bob,
You make books
come alive. I like
to hear you read.

10-3-92

Rachel K.

9-16-92

TWO

Theory into Practice: What Is Whole Language?

Principals are hearing a lot about whole language these days—both from teachers who want support and from central office administrators who are mandating for or against whole language in schools. Some principals know about whole language from their own teaching experiences, university classes, or classroom-based research. Others do not have any of these experiences on which to ground the decisions they make with their teachers and staff in sound educational principles. Most principals want to judge for themselves the validity of holistic teaching and learning.

What Whole Language Is

All school programs, curriculums, and teaching methods build on a particular view of learning. The predominant view has been based on behaviorist research conducted (primarily with animals) early in the twentieth century. In this view, students are believed to learn from part to whole. They are expected to learn letters and sounds before words and sentences, and then they are drilled to be certain that they "get it." Students are filled with facts and skills transmitted by all-knowing adults.

This behaviorist model has led to "teacher-proof" templates for sequencing direct instruction in skills, as exemplified by traditional basal reading programs, and to standardized multiple-choice and fill-in-the-blank tests as the means for assessment.

Whole language builds on Piaget's (1965) *constructivist* theory of learning. Constructivists describe learning as an active process in which children interact with adults and other children in authentic settings. Children construct their own knowledge through approximating, practicing, and interacting with knowledgeable others (Vygotsky 1977). To maximize the opportunities for student learning, adults organize the environment to facilitate dialogue, demonstrate or model the processes and concepts, provide support for learning, and evaluate or assess.

Most commonly, the term *whole language* refers to how listening, speaking, reading, and writing are learned and taught at school. It is a more inclusive view of learning and teaching. The research of Goodman (1970), Goodman and Goodman (1979), Taylor (1983), Harste and Short with Burke (1995), and others (Britton et al. 1975; Clark 1975; Graves 1975; Gollasch 1982; Harste, Burke, and Woodward 1984; Lindfors 1987) has clearly demonstrated that students develop literacy through reading and writing whole texts for real purposes. According to Ken Goodman in *What's Whole in Whole Language?* (1986), "It's a way of bringing together a view of language, a view of learning, and a view of people, in particular two special groups of people: kids and teachers" (5). Some of the principles of whole language that have emerged from this body of language development research include:

- Listening, speaking, reading, and writing are interrelated language processes that are learned in similar ways.
- Understanding and comprehension are always the goals of language learning.
- Language learning and thinking occur through social interactions that have personal meaning and purpose for each student.
- Oral and written language develop from whole to part and include the concepts of sounds, letters, sentence patterns, and meaning.
- Language loses meaning when it is taken out of context.
- Students learn best when their language development and knowledge are respected and form the basis for further learning.
- Students learn when they are in an atmosphere that allows them to take risks and learn from their mistakes.
- There is no guaranteed one-to-one correspondence between what an adult teaches and what students learn; students construct their own understandings built on their past experiences and knowledge.

What Whole Language Is Not

Like many educational innovations, whole language has become a buzzword, even a fad. It takes on varied meanings with each speaker or school district (Edelsky, Altwerger, and Flores 1991). Since whole language seems so difficult to visualize, it sometimes seems easier to define what it is not:

- It is not a method, and there is no one way to "do" whole language. As whole language has become more accepted, publishers and school district personnel have labeled many programs as holistic, naturalistic, or whole language and have expected teachers to follow a prescribed agenda. This defeats the ideas behind whole language: that learning builds on students' existing schemas and interests, districts' curriculums, and teachers' knowledge of their students and teaching/learning strategies.

- It is not a program and cannot be packaged. Every student and class is unique. A prescribed program will not work in every setting. Teachers use their judgment, knowledge, and experience to organize the learning environment for their students. Teachers are accountable for their teaching and students are accountable for their learning. Materials don't teach. Materials are used by good teachers to support learning.

- It is not the same as open classrooms, and students are not left to their own devices to "wander through a garden of print." Literacy and oral language strategy lessons and minilessons are important parts of the school day.

- Teachers are not laissez-faire, unfocused, or lazy; students are not undisciplined. While their classrooms are very busy and talk and interaction are the norm, good whole language teachers plan thoroughly, continually reflecting on individual student and group needs. From the first day of the school year, teachers provide structures, plans, and opportunities for students to learn based on ongoing assessment that informs daily instructional decisions.

- It is not necessarily a literature based reading program. Quality literature (fiction and nonfiction) and reference materials are basic to a whole language classroom, but the "basalization" of literature and the reduction of responses to literature to predetermined worksheets and workbooks are not consistent with whole language philosophy.

- Whole language is inherently neither easy nor difficult to implement. It does require that teachers put into practice their knowledge of language-learning principles, curriculum, teaching/learning strategies, child development, and materials and resources. Teachers have the professional responsibility to know how to fit materials to the needs of their students. This responsibility makes some teachers uncomfortable. They are used to having materials laid out for them and are then able to blame the materials or (too often) the children when things don't go well.

Language-Learning Principles

Brian Cambourne, in *The Whole Story* (1988), shows that learning the oral form and learning the written form of language are similar in many ways. Just as young children learn to speak the language of their homes through authentic interactions with loving family members, most learn to read and write at school by interacting with supportive, caring teachers. Cambourne lists the conditions necessary for natural learning as immersion, demonstration, engagement, expectation, approximation, use, and response.

Immersion

At home, young children are **immersed** in the oral language they are expected to learn. They grow up speaking just like the speakers with whom they are raised. A baby from Southeast Asia may be adopted by a family in Atlanta, Georgia, and grow up speaking with a southern United States dialect. The same baby would speak differently if adopted and raised by a family in Brooklyn, New York; Bangor, Maine; Paris, France; or Munich, Germany.

Some children are also immersed in functional print at home, print that fulfills a variety of purposes and that changes for different audiences. Parents may read to them from the Bible or picture books at bedtime. Children may see family members writing lists, letters, or bills. Cereal boxes, milk containers, and other food items all contain print labels, and favorite restaurants are easily identifiable by their printed logos and signs.

*At school, teachers **immerse** their students in print. Students interact with books and other materials, as well as with their teachers and other readers and writers. Signs, labels, lists, diagrams, charts, and graphs that emerge from children's literature studies and inquiry projects are displayed around the room, along with fiction, nonfiction, reference materials, and environmental print from the community.*

Demonstration

Family members **demonstrate** what language sounds like, how language is used with different audiences, and how it may be tied to actions and other language in purposeful situations. They see that their caretakers use different language when talking to the minister or rabbi than when they speak to their friends.

*At school, teachers and other students **demonstrate** how reading and writing are used. Teachers read and write in front of their students to illustrate how literacy is used for recreational and communicative purposes. Teachers are deliberate in their "thinking out loud" in order to illustrate how proficient readers and writers think. Frequently teachers say to themselves, Let's see, what is another way to write that? or Where could I go to find out more about that?*

Engagement

Young children **engage** in language learning at home when they see that they can accomplish a task successfully and that it has purpose in their lives. They also need to see that they are safe to make mistakes without incurring negative reactions.

*Students **engage** in literacy learning in classrooms that are safe, where teachers encourage risk taking, and where literacy is viewed as attainable and purposeful. Children participate in oral and written conversations in a variety of contexts and groupings. For example, students work in large groups, in small cooperative groups, with reading/writing partners in their classrooms, or as cross-age/peer coaches.*

Expectation

Children **expect** to learn the language they hear around them. Parents, grandparents, and other caretakers also assume that their children will be efficient users of the home language.

*Everyone in the classroom **expects** that students are becoming efficient readers and writers because each child is recognized as a reader and writer from the beginning. Teachers help children gain confidence in their own abilities and empower them to become responsible and accountable for their own learning.*

Approximation

Young children **approximate** the language they hear. They are not expected to speak perfectly from the beginning. Adults learning new activities also approximate. Professional athletes, experienced quilters, and master chefs continue to approximate their goals.

*Students **approximate** the written language around them. Approximations are encouraged in their spellings and in their attempts at reading or writing new genres. Teachers recognize that "one report does not a good report writer make" and provide many opportunities for inquiry in the classroom as children grow as researchers. The expectation is that given time and a variety of literacy experiences with a knowledgeable teacher, conventional forms of reading and writing will develop.*

Use

Young children need time and opportunity to **use** their developing knowledge of language at home. Ruth Weir (1962) describes how her infant son used the sounds of language over and over again at night in his crib, almost as if he were rehearsing a form of his newly learned oral language.

*Reading and writing need to be **in use** throughout the school day in all areas of the curriculum. Children cannot gain fluency in reading and writing*

without reading and writing every day. They cannot wait to know all the let-
ters and sounds before they begin writing. They need daily opportunities to
read other's writing and try out their own strategies and ideas for what they
think literacy is.

Response

Parents and others around the learner **respond** to their developing knowledge
of language and expand on it. Adults rarely correct toddlers' newly developing
speech. After hearing a three-year-old say, "I goed to Grandma's," a parent is
likely to respond, "Yes, you went to Grandma's yesterday and played all day.
What did you like best at Grandma's house?"

*Teachers **respond** to and expand students' language learning. They aim*
their responses at what the children are trying to do, rather than solely at the
product. Approximations are recognized as the child's best attempt at that
time.

Reading and Writing at Home

At home, young children may generalize their knowledge of the tube of toothpaste in their bathroom to the print in an ad for that brand of toothpaste in a
magazine by using the picture, the print, or a combination of both. Children
who are read to at home hear a story over and over again and may appear to
memorize the text. Research done by Myna (Haussler 1982) and others indicate
that this memorization is a beginning or emergent step in learning to read.

Many children in our literate society have writing experiences before starting school. In fact, most of us tell "scribbling" stories about the young children
we know. Children watch their grandma writing a shopping list and take their
own paper to write a list, whether or not it looks like writing to grandma. If
they cannot find paper, they write on anything they find, even walls. Harste,
Burke, and Woodward (1984) have examples of children as young as two or
three who differentiate between their "writing" and "drawing" where one
always is circular movements and the other is always linear movements.

Dolores Durkin (1966), in her landmark study of children who learned to
read before formal schooling, found that the homes of these children have several important features in common:

- Young readers are surrounded by a variety of print materials.
- Someone in the household uses copious amounts of print for a variety of
  purposes.
- Young readers have access to writing materials at an early age and are
  encouraged to use them.

■   Someone in the household responds to the child's attempts at reading and writing as authentic.

These elements that support early literacy development have been corroborated by the later research of Bill Teale and Elizabeth Sulzby (1986).

Reading and Writing at School

These same literacy principles are at work at school. Students match their past experiences with texts and content to read and write both familiar and new texts.

Authenticity is a driving concept for whole language teachers and administrators. Researchers such as Edelsky and Smith (1984) maintain that authentic language experiences occur when students communicate genuine responses to real audiences. Based on his own classroom research, Bob finds authenticity "reflected in the individual's choice to create and share meaningful and purposeful text for a self-selected audience" (Wortman 1990, 311).

A comparison of two writing experiences illustrates the concept of authenticity:

First-grade children complete a workbook page on parts of a letter.
First-grade children write thank-you notes to the principal for reading them her favorite book.

Both experiences involve functional use of letter writing, but there are essential differences that lie at the heart of authenticity: the letter written to the principal communicates a genuine response to an actual event for a real audience.

In noninstructional settings, all writers have a specific context, purpose, and audience in mind. The relationship to that context, audience, and purpose determines the format of the writing and the words the writer uses. Reading or writing a letter is different from reading or writing a grocery list, a poem, a novel, a report, or a set of directions. Reading or writing a letter is different if the writer or audience is your mother, your minister, your best friend, or your superintendent.

Traditionally, reading at school has been seen as a process whereby the sounds and letters of the author's text must be decoded by the reader to be understood. In the whole language view of reading, the reader brings prior knowledge and experience about the world and how language works to the reading process. Making meaning of the text is more important than decoding the letters and sounds of the text. Readers connect individual knowledge and experience to what they read, and when they connect their understandings with the author's text, they "transact" meaning with the author (Rosenblatt 1978). Thus, two people can read the same text and come away with two different ideas.

A major public misconception (and one often found within the educational community as well) is that whole language instruction does not include phonics. It does. To read and write in an alphabetic system such as English students must understand the sound/letter relationships. But it is not necessary to teach every sound individually over and over for it to be learned. The "pieces of language" like letters and sounds must always be tied to a meaningful context. If five-year-old Zachary wants to know more about *z* than about *b*, he shouldn't have to wait through twenty weeks of kindergarten before he can.

Reading in a whole language class occurs all day long as teachers organize opportunities for students to engage in authentic literacy experiences. These opportunities arise as children interact with songs, poetry, thematic vocabulary charts, dictionaries, recipes, literature books, and textbooks.

Student-generated writing also supports reading. Children see that they can write down their thoughts, feelings, or knowledge for others to read, just as they read the thoughts, feelings, or knowledge of other authors. This promotes clear purposes for writing and supports children's developing sense of audience. Writing is also a vehicle for children to make connections between words and letters and their meanings, sounds, and appearance.

Writing in journals is a personal reflection of students' lives; writing in learning logs, such as literature or mathematics logs, is a personal response to or documentation of student learning. The content or meaning of these types of personal writing is paramount; usually little or no attention needs to be given to the mechanics of writing within these contexts. Outside of school we don't edit our diaries and personal journals because we are our own audience.

Writing for other purposes, especially writing for audiences outside the classroom, involves attention to an editing process that includes both content and mechanics. This writing process is described at length by Donald Graves (1983), Lucy Calkins (1986), and others. It includes using writing as a tool for thinking and communicating. Children need choices in their topics for writing and to revise and edit drafts that will be published for others to read. Teachers therefore work to support children in many authentic contexts for going public with their writing.

Whole language teachers and principals use their knowledge of how literacy works to develop, assess, and support students' learning strategies. They recognize that adults can't waste precious classroom time getting students ready to read, ready to write, ready for first grade, or ready for middle school. Whole language teachers and principals put their commitment and energies into identifying students' areas of strength and building on them in authentic and meaningful contexts. To paraphrase John Dewey ([1938] 1972), they believe that education isn't preparation for life; education is life.

Teaching happens in the minds of teachers. If we want instruction to change, we have to support teachers in changing their transmissional views of the learning process.

MonDay   I like How
Hi   Mr Wortman.
you Be the PrencaBell.
And. I like How you look
You look good in the close
And I like you to.
Wat Book are you
Reading My FraVret Book
is the greety goat.
From Michuel

24

THREE

What Does a Whole Language Classroom Look Like?

Principals and teachers are often frustrated because they cannot find easy answers to this question. While there is no template for the best whole language classroom, there are common features. When organizing for whole language, principals and teachers can base their decisions on these common considerations.

The Vital Role of the Principal

Just as teachers build on their students' knowledge to extend learning in teachable moments, whole language principals take advantage of learning opportunities in their day-to-day interactions with the adults in their schools. We support our teachers in developing and sustaining whole language classrooms by:

- Observing and offering suggestions.
- Demonstrating and bringing in resource people to demonstrate.
- Co-planning.
- Rolling up our sleeves.
- Providing resources.
- Involving teachers in their own professional development.

Observing and Offering Suggestions

By observing and discussing what is happening in classrooms, a principal provides important information to teachers who are making changes in their thinking and classroom organization. Observers often see differently than teachers do, and whole language principals make wonderful observers. The lessons we learned as collaborators in our own classroom research have influenced our thinking as principals. Years ago when Myna was conducting research in Bob's classroom, we found that she had a broader picture of what was going on in the room at any one time. As the teacher, Bob was focused on what the children were learning or how lessons were going. As a trusted observer, Myna was able to pose important questions that helped Bob reflect on his practice.

When principals make suggestions in a nonthreatening way, teachers can build on their suggestions. This implies, of course, that teachers trust the principal and believe they really are a team working together to help children learn. The classroom of a teacher new to Borton was always cluttered with stacks of student work that needed to be completed, displayed, or filed in student writing folders. Bob also noticed that the teacher was spending her after-school planning time cleaning up the room. Specifically observing centers and cleanup time in her room, Bob saw that the teacher was so intent on her work with children that she left only a few minutes for them to clean up, then she would finish cleaning for them. Rather than berate her for her messy classroom, Bob said, "I notice that you are so focused on the students during their work period that cleanup time is often very rushed. An important part of students' learning is becoming responsible for completing their work and that includes cleaning up. When students are responsible for maintaining materials in the room, it gives you more time for the important work of planning. How can you build in opportunities for students to be responsible for keeping the classroom organized?"

After some discussion and brainstorming with Bob and another of her colleagues, this teacher:

- Implemented writing folders in which the students filed their own work.
- Organized materials such as scissors, crayons, markers, and paper in tubs that were easily accessible and labeled.
- Asked classroom helpers to set out and maintain the needed materials each day.
- Built in times during the day for all her students to clean up.

This far surpassed Bob's expectations. This outstanding teacher made changes that went beyond any she might have made had Bob directed her to "tidy up" her classroom.

Sometimes checklists can be effective, if they are individualized, adapted to the community's purposes, and designed to help teachers reflect on their practices. Bob occasionally uses a simple checklist that helps teachers zero in on the elements of a literate environment. He finds it a useful basis for talking with teachers new to whole language and to the challenges of working with a diverse community of learners. Here is his checklist:

Evidences of a Positive Language-Learning Environment:

1. What in the room encourages/invites/promotes/facilitates oral language development?
2. What in the room encourages/invites/promotes/facilitates reading?
3. What in the room encourages/invites/promotes/facilitates writing?
4. What utensils/resources are easily accessible to children for literacy activities?
5. What in the room illustrates the relationship between talking, writing, and reading?
6. What in the room reflects/promotes languages or dialects other than standard English that may be spoken by all or some of the children?
7. What in the room fosters understanding of and respect for the cultural diversity of your community?

Myna adapted a checklist developed by Principal Rosanna Gallagher for observing classrooms (see Figure 3.1). The checklist provides a snapshot of how the classroom is organized for teaching and learning.

Some whole language advocates believe that checklists are static and cannot give a complete picture of classrooms. We certainly acknowledge that checklists are only one source of data for decision making and that no one checklist is applicable in all cases. That is why we continue to modify our own and others' checklists, and we invite you to rework ours.

Demonstrating and Bringing in Resource People to Demonstrate

As Cambourne states in *The Whole Story: Natural Learning and the Acquisition of Literacy in the Classroom* (1988), demonstration is a strong support for learning. We use demonstration to support teachers as they learn new teaching and learning strategies. Bob is very comfortable demonstrating lessons and literacy interactions. An experienced teacher, he shows other teachers how to organize the activities to build on children's existing knowledge and expand their learning.

Myna prefers to offer suggestions and to bring in other resource people to provide demonstrations, especially when teachers request help. Sometimes district resource people and university professors are invited to demonstrate a range of teaching and learning strategies. Teachers at Warren are especially open to demonstrating areas of strengths to their colleagues and learning from one another. One of Myna's most successful strategies has been to free teachers by taking over their classes for short periods or hiring a substitute for a full day so they may observe their colleagues. This peer observation has not only given

Principal/Teacher Feedback Checklist

Teacher: _____   T. A.: _____

Date: _____   Time: _____

TEACHER
- ❑ Reading to students
- ❑ Working with small group of students
- ❑ Assessing student understanding (observation, question, evaluation activity)
- ❑ Presenting a lesson to total group
- ❑ Demonstrating
- ❑ Leading a class discussion
- ❑ Walking around room
- ❑ Sitting at desk
- ❑ Listening with students to _____
- ❑ Working with another adult _____
- ❑ Other _____

STUDENT
- ❑ Involved in small group (partner) centers, cooperative groups
- ❑ Involved in total group activity
- ❑ All students working independently on same/similar activity
- ❑ All students working independently on variety of activities
- ❑ Peer teaching/sharing
- ❑ Presenting (play, puppet show, etc.)
- ❑ Discussing
- ❑ Listening
- ❑ Other _____

TEACHER ASSISTANT
- ❑ Working with small group
- ❑ Working with individual student
- ❑ Working in teaming situation with teacher
- ❑ Walking around room assisting students
- ❑ Doing paperwork
- ❑ Other _____

MATERIALS USED BY STUDENTS
- ❑ Charts
- ❑ Teacher made
- ❑ Student made
- ❑ Tapes
- ❑ Trade books
- ❑ Hands on materials
- ❑ Magazines
- ❑ Paper, pencils, crayons, etc.
- ❑ Textbook
- ❑ Workbook
- ❑ Dittos
- ❑ Chalkboard
- ❑ Maps
- ❑ Kit
- ❑ Other _____

- ❑ Parent in room working

Figure 3.1   Principal/Teacher Feedback Checklist.

teachers ideas and the extra boost to change but also built strong respect among the teachers.

Co-planning

Planning is the hardest part of whole language teaching. It involves keeping the big picture in mind—knowing what the mandated curriculum requires and understanding how students learn best based on child development and learning theory. Planning also requires flexibility, because these important elements must be meshed with students' interests and current knowledge. World and local events also shape curriculum and divert plans into new directions. For example, a few years ago the events surrounding Desert Storm shaped geography and history lessons, literature studies, and letter-writing experiences at both schools.

Whole language principals, experienced in planning and equipped with a global view of curriculum and students, sit down with teachers and encourage long-term planning and assessment. Talking through plans helps teachers conceptualize and focus their thoughts. It helps principals understand what teachers have in mind. When we plan with teachers, we gain insight into their thinking and we can use the opportunity to expand their thinking.

A strategy particularly helpful for long-term planning is webbing, a pictorial representation of brainstormed ideas. Principals can help teachers define the various components of the web, such as expected student learning, themes, strategies, materials, and time lines. Myna encourages teachers at Warren to do long-term planning. She asks for quarterly overviews of their goals and expectations for student learning. Webbing is an easy way for her to sit down with teachers and help them plan out quarterly goals and theme studies.

Rolling Up Our Sleeves

Sometimes supporting a teacher just involves saying, "Okay, let's see what it looks like. Do you want help moving these desks around?" Seeing their principal actively try out new arrangements, strategies, and theories can provide that extra boost some teachers need to make their own changes. When the librarian at Warren needed new expensive shelving for the library, Myna put on her blue jeans and went with him to scout through the basement and attic of an old school to find shelves that worked just fine.

Providing Resources

Sometimes money, time, and new materials are what it takes to support change. These definitely are areas where principals can make a difference. It's where we can show our commitment through "begging."

When Myna came to Warren, teachers told her that students needed tables for collaborative groupings, that the old desks could not be easily grouped or moved. It was a hard decision. She wanted to buy new furniture, but the school library needed books. Myna was not deterred. She telephoned her assistant superintendent and the district director of purchasing, reminding them how long it had been since Warren classrooms had any new furnishings and providing educational reasons for needing new tables and chairs. Because Myna "begged," enough money was found that first year to upgrade two classrooms and begin building the library collection.

Myna and Bob also encourage teachers and parents to join them in writing grant proposals. Borton teachers and students were becoming very interested in environmental education and wanted to turn a vacant lot adjacent to the school into an urban wildlife habitat. Bob found a parent who was willing to write a proposal asking the Arizona Department of Fish and Game for $4,000 to create the "Borton Bird Sanctuary." Receiving the grant was the impetus Bob and others needed to request additional funds from community agencies to expand the project. So far Borton has received almost $30,000 in grants and in-kind services and materials for this project.

Involving Teachers in Their Own Professional Development

We apply the same principles of learning that we hold for students to the adults with whom we work and to ourselves. Adults will resist learning new strategies and information when they are mandated to accept change. They will initiate change when it is authentic and has meaning to them. This topic of professional development is fully addressed in Chapter 6.

Considerations That Shape Whole Language Classrooms

As whole language principals we do not make decisions unilaterally; we collaborate with others to support learning and instruction. We see our most important role as getting students, parents, and staff involved in the daily decisions that affect the school.

The most important decisions teachers make relate to the organization of their classrooms to support student learning. Teachers' decisions are based on many factors:

- Background knowledge and experiences.
- Physical setting and organizing to learn.
- Grouping students to learn.
- Literate environment.
- Integrated curriculum.
- Social and emotional climate.

Background Knowledge and Experiences

Everyone has areas of strength that are unique starting places for learning. Learning and change are never painless, but they occur more smoothly when we identify and build on existing knowledge and strengths. When working with teachers, we try not to change everything at once or respond negatively to their current practice. Bob builds on the teaching staff's strengths when he takes visitors around the school and points out positive aspects of each classroom.

Teachers who hear their principal talking about their accomplishments to visitors believe that he really means it.

What makes a good whole language teacher is not a particular style of teaching, a room arrangement, a reading loft or animals in the classroom, or even a formal spelling program. Each teacher is unique and becomes an outstanding teacher only when he or she can find a personal voice. Vera Milz, an exceptionally gifted first-grade teacher in Bloomfield, Michigan, who has been a pioneer in the whole language movement, is quick to point out to other teachers that it's okay to be a whole language teacher who doesn't "sing or dance."

Principals often "discover" an outstanding whole language teacher who has been spotlighted at a conference or been recommended by a colleague, and they then visit that classroom intent on replicating the learning environment in their school. The problem is, every whole language community takes on the personality of the adults and children who come together to share their days. It is not possible to replicate another teacher's classroom or another principal's school.

Outstanding whole language teachers have classrooms that are unique from other whole language teachers because classrooms take on the personality of the teachers and students who call them home. This social construction is basic to an understanding of how classrooms work (Whitmore and Crowell 1994).

To promote a holistic learning environment, it is necessary to maintain teachers' autonomy and to appreciate and support everyone's strengths. Good teachers, no matter their beliefs, generally share the common goal of wanting students to love learning. Almost all teachers are providing the best education they know how, and to be critical of their efforts would undermine their confidence and enthusiasm. There is something positive to build on in almost every class. If not, it is the administrator's responsibility to work with the teacher or, in extreme cases, institute the documentation process necessary for dismissal.

Myna has had whole language teachers ask why she "allows" other teachers in the building to continue using strategies that obviously come from a skills model rather than a more holistic stance. She explains that if she truly believes in whole language principles, she must acknowledge and build on the strengths of all teachers. She reminds these less patient teachers that while they were quick to jump into change, they must be more patient with their colleagues who may be more skeptical, methodical, or deliberate.

It is often easiest to begin fostering change in writing, social studies, science, or literature, because teachers frequently have interests or strengths in one of these areas. To our dismay, we have been more successful in encouraging wary teachers by suggesting an "adding on" approach, as much as we know that is *not* the best way to initiate long-term classroom change. Nevertheless, when teachers in our schools tried adding one new facet to their curricular approach, they reflected on student responses and learning in that one area. Often the excitement and progress of their students made them consider including these new strategies permanently. It was then that we encouraged the teachers to let at least one other less successful teaching and learning strategy go.

Myna encouraged Thomas, whose students wrote often, to have them write more than one draft, so they could get their ideas down quickly and then revise to be sure that their audience would understand what they had written. When Thomas was talking about the growth his students were making in writing now that they were writing more than one draft, Myna asked to see the students' work. Together Myna and Thomas discussed the refinement of the students' thoughts on successive drafts. Myna also asked if he would be interested in talking to a university consultant about the writing process and his students' revisions. Although he did not say yes, Myna continues to support his efforts in having students revise their writing. She continues to ask occasionally whether he wants additional support to accomplish the changes he is initiating. Even now, Thomas continues to reflect and refine his own thinking about the writing process.

Physical Setting and Organizing to Learn

The layout and amount of space limit the ways in which a classroom can be organized. So do windows, doors, sinks, and electrical outlets. Classrooms are never big enough; they never have enough storage space or bookcases. Using existing space is critical to whole language teaching and learning, so both teachers and students must be ingenious and creative. *The Whole Language Catalogue* (Goodman, Bird, and Goodman 1991) and *Organizing for Whole Language* (Goodman, Hood, and Goodman 1991) are two good starting points for organizing the physical layout of whole language classrooms. Figures 3.2 and 3.3 illustrate representative primary and intermediate whole language classrooms at Borton and Warren Schools. Classrooms are organized to promote and support student learning in a variety of contexts consistent with the goals discussed in Chapter 4.

Access to materials is important. Students need to be able to function without constant assistance from their teacher. If teachers' interactions with groups of students are continually interrupted because the teacher is the sole dispenser of materials such as paper and pencils, a great deal of learning time is wasted, and students do not develop a sense of classroom ownership and responsibility. In our schools' classrooms writing materials—pens, pencils, crayons, markers, paint, and various types of lined and unlined paper—are readily available. Baskets or bins are placed around the room or in a specifically designated writing center.

We are supportive when teachers extend the concept of floor space in their classrooms to include other areas. We suggest raising platforms as quiet reading lofts. Hanging art displays and charts from ceilings conserves scarce bulletin board and wall space. Areas of movement, activity, and noise are kept

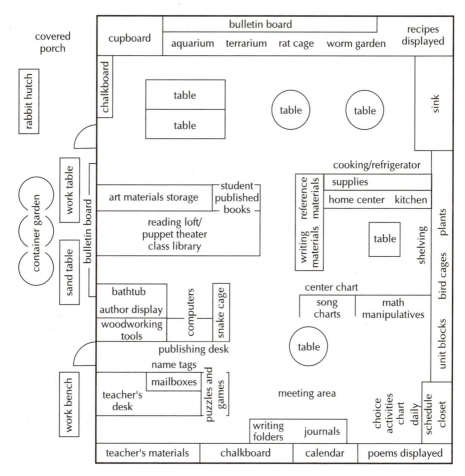

Figure 3.2 Sample arrangement of a primary whole language classroom.

away or sectioned off from areas reserved for quieter activities (browsing in the class library, for example). Sometimes teachers can expand classroom space by moving noisy or messy activities onto a patio or into a hallway.

Paints are stored near sinks to facilitate cleanup, and pails or basins serve when sinks are not available. Cooking or science areas are best set up near sinks and appliances when possible. Small hot plates may be added when needed. Immovable light sources and receptacles may be augmented with a few extension cords. Masonite boards, white laminate boards, and large and small chalkboards provide writing surfaces when space is limited.

Flooring, whether carpet, linoleum, or tile, affects the type of materials and activities that work more effectively and the amount of cleanup required. Specific spaces can be defined and extended with rugs, carpet squares, larger

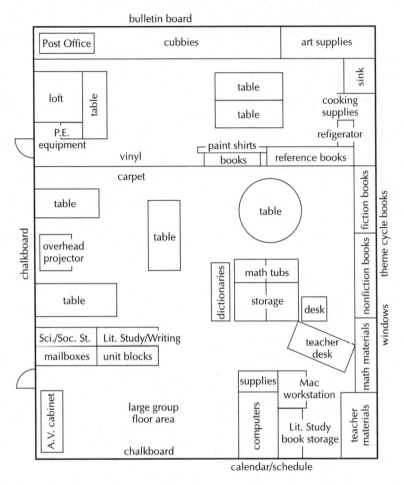

Figure 3.3   Sample arrangement of an intermediate whole language classroom.

pieces of carpeting, or pieces of linoleum to allow for extra meeting, science, cooking, block-building, or art areas. Platform risers have many uses, including group meetings, performances, work spaces, and conversation areas. Teacher Gloria Kaufman has a pattern for wooden risers that friends, including Myna's husband, have helped her build. Before she got the wooden risers, Gloria carried her school's metal chorus risers into her room every day. Principals can help teachers acquire these resources through donations or creative budgeting.

Selecting appropriate furniture offers further options for facilitating learning. We help our teachers group desks or tables to provide space for social interactions, group work, and discussion. Tables take up less space than individual desks. Round tables offer more flexibility than rectangular ones in tight spaces. Shelves can be used as room dividers or activity boundaries and at the same time hold materials for specific tasks. Chart racks not only offer additional display space but also provide added privacy.

Grouping Students to Learn

Holistic environments are organized so that children have space to learn in a variety of social groupings. Groupings should vary with the social context and learning purposes: whole group or large groups, small groups, pairs, or individuals. We remind teachers that grouping decisions are based on student needs.

In large groups, students can use peers as individual resources while at the same time draw on group support. For some children, it is easier to take risks with a smaller group or one special friend than in front of the entire class.

Small groups change frequently depending on their purposes. Sometimes teachers group students homogeneously for specific ministrategy lessons: left-to-right directionality or predicting from prior knowledge, for example. More often than not, however, heterogeneous groupings serve students' needs best, because less experienced students learn from their more proficient classmates. Proficient students benefit from the opportunity to explain their understandings to less experienced peers.

The classroom must also provide opportunities for students to work alone and to become self-sufficient and self-evaluating. On their own, children may think through and extend knowledge learned in group settings. These thoughtful and reflective periods require space somewhat removed from the usual distractions of a busy classroom.

Literate Environment

To become proficient readers and writers, children need access to a wide range of literacy materials. Whole language teachers select literacy materials for the purposes or functions they serve and the space and preparation required for their use. Children read for real purposes from a variety of texts, including nonfiction, fiction, and reference materials like encyclopedias, atlases, and thesauruses.

In holistic classrooms, trade books, textbooks, attendance charts, group graphs, webs, lists, recipes, song charts, signs and labels, and other writing genres are available as resources for ideas and spelling. "Pieces of language" such as letters of the alphabet, parts of speech, and vocabulary are not taught outside functional contexts. Kindergartners learn about the sound of *J* when they find all the *J* names on name cards and in poem and song charts in their room. Writing resources, such as charts and lists, are deliberately placed at eye level and consciously used by the teacher as demonstrations for pupils in their functional writing or other tasks.

In classrooms with a variety of writing implements, art supplies, and types of paper at hand, students use these resources more frequently and write more freely (Loughlin and Martin 1984). Dialogue journals, response logs, research reports, poetry, planning charts, brainstormed lists, and other writing become tools for learning about the world. Fourth graders learn about alphabetical order when they use the card catalogue in their research.

We encourage teachers to replace the disconnected and isolated activities of traditional textbooks by letting them use money that is normally budgeted for workbooks to buy trade books and other instructional materials. We also encourage teachers to visit other classrooms to observe collaborative and personalized activities that scaffold learning with other subject matter areas and with students' life experiences. Bob took over a writers workshop in Susan's class for forty-five minutes while she observed another teacher beginning a new thematic unit and saw a new "what we know and what we want to find out" brainstorming strategy in action.

Teachers and students have collaborative roles in holistic classes. Classrooms are organized to support this collaborative work and encourage students to demonstrate their knowledge. The daily interactions with written language involve a variety of experiences and materials as well as teaching/learning and kidwatching strategies. The environment allows for and invites immersion in planned oral and written language experiences. It offers enough depth to encourage concentration and enough breadth to involve all children within the range of their experience and development.

Integrated Curriculum

The daily curriculum of the classroom—what is taught, studied, and learned—is a match between state- and district-mandated courses of study, teacher-initiated programs and themes, and student purposes and needs. Supported by the early work of John Dewey ([1938] 1972) and Hilda Taba (1966), some teachers have integrated the curriculum to make learning more social, concrete, and meaningful for their students. These approaches are often based on a social studies theme or unit, such as transportation or survival, and students actively research answers to their questions and undertake projects related to the topic. Inversely, content areas are often considered positive vehicles for supporting language and literacy development.

Current brain research supports holistic learning strategies, including integrating content areas, because the brain connects with and builds on existing knowledge or schemas. The brain continually seeks to make sense out of the world. If new knowledge doesn't connect and make sense, it is discarded and never learned. Therefore, the connections between discrete facts and ideas are the best means for organizing classroom curriculums. Learners need to explore ideas and concepts through a variety of sign systems, such as music, art, and dance, not rely solely on language to develop greater understanding. Armed with over twenty-five years of research on how we learn and how our brains function, Carol Edelsky, Bess Altwerger, and Barbara Flores (1991), Susan Kovalik and Karen Olsen (1994), Mary Ann and Gary Manning and Roberta Long (1994), and other educators are actively promoting thematic instruction as a powerful means of making curriculum accessible to students.

In his article "The Futility of Trying to Teach Everything of Importance," Grant Wiggins (1989) reminds us that we can't possibly teach every discrete skill, workbook page, end-of-chapter test, and "piece" of learning laid out in state and district curriculums—even if we tried. He also points out the faulty logic in assuming that all learning occurs through direct instruction. These are the two basic principles on which the concept of integrating curriculum is based.

Integrating curriculum means organizing classroom studies around broad concepts that support learning by connecting students' past experiences with new knowledge. Teachers and students work together, negotiating thematic studies that center around authentic questions. The traditional boundaries between science, social studies, fine arts, humanities, and mathematics are broken down and all these areas are used to support students' inquiry. The language arts are tools for learning, and the inquiry process becomes the focal point of the curriculum. Teachers gather materials, plan and organize experiences, and develop specific learning strategies that will best support student learning. They decide what is best learned through integrated themes, direct teaching, guest speakers, literature, project work, or other means.

A balanced curriculum is maintained because teachers make decisions about what subjects, strategies, or information is needed by their specific group of students. Every subject need not be included just for the sake of integration. For instance, when Lindsey's class was reading *The Wall* by Eve Bunting (1990) as part of a theme cycle on conflict, the students figured out how many years ago the United States was involved in Viet Nam and drew time lines to scale. Lindsey integrated mathematics into that particular theme, but Myna does not expect her to integrate mathematics into every theme. Myna knows that Lindsey is knowledgeable about mathematics and that she provides many additional opportunities for students to learn math.

In *Creating Classrooms for Authors and Inquirers* (1995), Jerry Harste, Kathy Short, and Carolyn Burke have taken a bold step in looking at the authoring cycle as a framework for developing theme studies that have real meaning and purpose for children. The cycle allows teachers to include all necessary concepts. Students assume the real roles that people play in society. They study the Westward Movement from the stance of historians, economists, diplomats, environmentalists, or painters. They study biomes from the perspective of ecologists, anthropologists, meteorologists, biologists, or geologists.

In holistic classrooms, teachers tap into the existing schemas of children and follow their lead into those questions that will engage and sustain their interest over time. Integrated curriculum is an important strategy by which students help select those concepts and ideas that most engage their interests and best connect them with the tools of learning—reading, writing, listening, and speaking. At the same time teachers continually ask themselves, Is this the best use of our students' time? What do students need to learn next and what is the best way to help them get there?

Classroom teachers who are knowledgeable kidwatchers and reflective practitioners are the best curriculum developers. They bring together their knowledge of curriculum, the learning and literacy processes, and their students to provide experiences that allow students to connect new knowledge and ideas with existing thinking. They build on students' knowledge and interest to involve students in their own learning process.

There are many packaged programs and basal materials that provide step-by-step instructions on how to organize concepts and activities important to specific themes. Most of these collections of activities are engagingly formatted attempts to transmit knowledge deemed important by experts. These sometimes provide starting places for teachers who have not had much experience with curriculum integration. The problem is that educators already spend a great deal of time answering questions that students don't have. Students remain passive in the process and integrated curriculum remains something that is done *to* them.

Some educators incorporate theme studies in the same way parents give children's birthday parties. They choose a theme (dinosaurs/bears/apples), gather all the props and plan the activities, decorate the room, put the children through the activities, provide coordinated plates, napkins, and cups, design a big final fun activity centered around the cake, send everyone home with matching party favors, take down the decorations, clean up, and go on to something else. No one, not even the birthday child, remembers very much.

We believe learning is the social construction of knowledge. We encourage teachers to give students the time to engage in learning, understand concepts, and rehearse new ideas until these things become part of their knowledge base. Most children can engage in functional and authentic learning activities for long periods. Even four- and five-year-olds can stick to learning tasks for an hour or more when they are actively engaged. How time is spent in classrooms shows what teachers value, and whole language teachers create integrated blocks of time for students to learn important concepts together. Figures 3.4 and 3.5 are samples of daily schedules.

Social and Emotional Climate

We talk in detail in the next chapter about the importance of establishing a safe social and emotional climate in which a community of learners can participate, take risks, and succeed. In whole language classrooms, just as at home, learning grows through social interactions—between teacher and student, student and teacher, and student and student. M. A. K. Halliday's 1977 view of language learning suggests a framework by which students learn the forms and functions

---

Possible Daily Schedule for Primary
Bob Wortman • Tucson Unified School District

8:30 A. M.	ESTABLISH COMMUNITY USSR/USSW/DEAR • Journals • Read To • Music • Energizer
8:45	COMMUNITY MEETING Morning "Stuff" • Business (calendar • lunch count • weather • review previous day • plan day)
9:15	LANGUAGE ARTS/SOCIAL STUDIES (M/W/F or T/TH combinations) (Large, small, paired, and individual groupings) Literature Study • Text Sets • Research • Projects • Journals • Unit Study • Shared/Guided Reading • Writers Workshop
10:45	FINE ARTS Music • Visual Arts • Sculpture • Drama
11:30	LUNCH Cafeteria Lines • Phone • Mail • Restroom • Meet with Principal (Maybe Eat)
12:15 P. M.	ESTABLISH COMMUNITY Read To • USSR/USSW/DEAR • Journals
12:30	SCIENCE/MATH (M/W/F or T/TH combinations) (Large, small, paired, and individual groupings) Problem Solving • Experiments • Manipulatives • Journals/Logs • Data Collection/Organization/Presentation • Projects • Shared/Guided Reading • Demonstrations • Unit Study
2:00	PHYSICAL EDUCTION Games • Creative Movement • Dance • Aerobics
2:30	SPECIALIST/COMPUTER LAB/AUTHOR'S CHAIR
3:00	COMMUNITY MEETING Review Day • Solve Problems • Assign Homework • Preview/Plan for Next Day
3:30	DISMISS

Figure 3.4 Sample primary whole language schedule.

of language. According to Halliday (1980) all individuals learn language, learn through language, and learn about language. In school, students learn to read, write, and speak; they learn the content of social studies, humanities, sciences, and mathematics through reading, writing, and oracy; and as they revise, rehearse, or are taught minilessons, they learn more about the language arts.

At home parents rarely correct a two- or three-year-old's grammar. Instead they scaffold or build on what the child is saying (Cazden 1988). Instead of saying, "That's wrong dear. You say, 'I don't have a cookie,' not 'I don't got no cookie,'" parents respond to the content of their child's message and demonstrate adult usage by saying, "I know you don't have a cookie. Would you like one?" Russian psychologist Lev Vygotsky (1977) called this a novice-expert view. Holistic classrooms provide the same type of scaffolding and support.

Possible Daily Schedule for Intermediate

Kathleen M. Crawford • Warren Elementary School

7:55 A. M.	FIRST BELL. Pick up students at south entrance (near kinder. class)
8:00	SECOND BELL. Students should all be in classroom. Meet on carpet for class meeting. Start by student taking attendance and lunch count. The class meeting monitor leads us in pledge, moment of silence, and joys and sorrows of the day. Students discuss problems and their solutions for getting along. Teacher will then go over class schedule for the day and other important agenda items. Finish meeting with a story/poem/song and lead into:
8:30	INDIVIDUAL QUIET READING TIME
9:00	WORK TIME. Includes literature/inquiry group discussions, writing workshop, individual assessment by teacher, open school library time, research, reading quietly or with others, or specific invitations as they are created by teacher and students.
10:15	PHYSICAL EDUCTION
10:30	MATH/SCIENCE WORKSHOP. Total class and small group experiences with math/science concepts. At least three days will be provided for menu selection of math activities.
11:30	LUNCH
12:05 P. M.	BELL. Pick up students at south-side entryway. Get drinks and meet on carpet for read aloud of a chapter book.
12:30	QUIET WRITING TIME. Students will work on individual writing while teacher meets with 5-6 students in a revising group to make goals with writing pieces for the week.
1:00	STUDIO TIME. This time may have a fine arts focus such as music, art, movement/dance, or drama; or it may be a continuation of work time if students need more time for writing, projects, book publishing, or individual inquiries.
1:45	LEARNING LOGS. Students will respond in logs on the day's happenings. What went well during the day? What problems happened? How did you participate in class today?
2:00	CLASS MEETING. Announcements needed for homework or the following day.
2:30	DISMISSAL
	BAND AND ORCHESTRA. Mondays and Fridays: adv. 9:30, beg. 10:00

Figure 3.5 Sample intermediate whole language schedule.

Whole language teachers plan and establish environments for risk taking and learning, demonstrate and extend the children's learning, and use assessment to determine the next step. They look for teachable moments, offering explanations rather than correcting errors. Years ago when Myna was observing in Bob's kindergarten/first-grade classroom, she watched a teachable moment involving six-year-old Allen. Her notes illustrate the safe climate Bob created so that his students could learn from other students and from him:

Allen voluntarily read his journal entry, and Bob wrote a response. Allen read Bob's response and wrote, "I like it *two*." Then he asked, "Is that the right *too*?" Bob spent several minutes pointing out the differences among *to, too,* and *two,* after which Allen changed his entry to read "*too.*". . . Over the next few days the spellings of *to, too,* and *two* were experimented with a great deal by a number of children who were operating at varying levels of literacy development and who had received no direct instruction. (Wortman and Matlin Haussler 1989)

Just as Bob set the tone in his whole language classroom for six-year-old Allen to take risks as a writer, we set the tone to support growth and change in our schools. We recognize that creating a climate that supports collaboration and risk taking is the first step in organizing a whole language school.

Dear
Mr. Wartman

I think every kid in
in the worlde should have
such a spacil pricadal
like you. you are the
Best Book reader and
reading is my favorit
subgect. I Have read
many book's I Have allway's
thout that my mam way's
the Best Boy whis i rong.

CHAPTER

FOUR

Building Community: Setting the Tone for Whole Language

For many years research and professional journals have treated principals as the instructional leaders of their schools. While the label is pervasive, the reality is often rhetorical. Instructional leadership needs to be manifested in the daily life of whole language principals. We believe that instructional leaders clearly demonstrate effective interactions to achieve their goals. Leaders plant the seeds, nurture and live their visions. Whole language principals must be comfortable in the role of master teachers in order to provide the participatory leadership necessary for a community to work collaboratively.

Our job as principals is to articulate, reflect on, and support the efforts of staff and parents so they constantly strive to live the school community's vision and meet its goals. We strive to make our goals implicit and explicit. Our personal actions are meant to set a standard or norm for building community in the school.

Personal Goals Impact the Community

It is important for administrators to be consistent in the implicit norms we value and also to be explicit in publishing personal goals for the school community. Going public with professional goals demands continual reflection and institutionalizes standards for the staff. The degree to which administrators maintain consistency in their beliefs and actions affects the emotional climate and the authenticity of the learning community. Each year we reflect on our previously published goals and revise and republish them within the school community and the district administration. Although they have become more refined over the years, the general tone of our individual professional goals tends to remain constant because of our strong beliefs about teaching and learning.

We publish our individual professional goals in different ways, depending on the audience (and Bob does it in both English and Spanish):

1. We discuss them with staff on the first day back after summer vacation.
2. We share them with parents in the first newsletter of the year.
3. We talk about them with the entire school community at open house and display them on special bulletin boards in public areas of the school.
4. We include them in our portfolios as part of our evaluation conferences with the assistant superintendent.
5. We display them in our offices on a big chart.

We have discussed our current personal goals and found them to be extremely similar, and we believe they are similar to those of many other whole language principals as well:

- Articulate a clear and consistent philosophy.
- Establish a safe emotional/social climate.
- Establish a collaborative environment.
- Focus instruction on learning.
- Promote a professional and scholarly focus.
- Work hard.
- Make school a place we enjoy returning to each day.
- Strengthen communication between school and home.

Articulate a Clear and Consistent Philosophy

As whole language principals, we believe it is important that what we say is in sync with what we do. We work to articulate our beliefs with courage and conviction to students, teachers, parents, superintendents, and community members at all times.

Just as we expect good teachers not to fill the day with disconnected activities that have little personal meaning to students, we as educational leaders do not automatically fill up our schedules with management tasks. We try to "practice what we teach" because we feel strongly that our actions set the vision, emotional climate, and expectations for students, parents, and staff. We make decisions thoughtfully and deliberately based on our personal goals; the shared school goals; our knowledge of learning theory, language learning, and child development; the strengths of individual staff members; and the unique social interactions of the school community. These decisions let the students, staff, and community know that we are professional educators well grounded in current research and practice.

We welcome the opportunity to collaborate and problem-solve with parents and staff rather than ignore or gloss over the hard questions that surface. Adherence to our own goals and beliefs plays a particularly powerful role as the "thread that runs so true," the lifeline that continually brings us back to the best interests of the school and children's learning.

Myna was recently approached by a couple who were upset because their daughter did not bring home traditional worksheets as their niece did at another school. They wanted Myna to "make sure that the teacher was teaching." Myna viewed her role as establishing clear communication and emphasizing the strengths she saw for the student's learning in this strong whole language class. Myna arranged a meeting for the parents, teacher, and herself. She gave the teacher the opportunity to explain her program and demonstrate how it met district-mandated curriculums. Myna also encouraged the parents to observe the classroom in action and accompanied them when they did, explaining what was occurring and the benefits of a classroom that worked this way.

Establish a Safe Emotional/Social Climate

Establishing a climate conducive to growth, creativity, and risk taking is one of our most important jobs as whole language principals. Current research on how the brain works maintains that "absence of threat" is critical to the learning process (Hart 1983). We have found we must be consistent and reflective in our actions with students, parents, and staff. People need to know what to expect.

Everyone benefits from being encouraged to grow. When the process of ongoing growth is acknowledged, we are less likely to dismiss a student, parent, or staff member as "impossible to work with" and "unable to change." We are committed to providing adults as well as children a safety net. If no one is willing to risk trying something new, learning becomes static. Everyone in the school community (especially teachers and principals) needs to feel that it is okay to "fail" before being willing to risk trying new strategies and more engaging activities.

Sometimes we bite our lips while teachers try out innovations because we are afraid we will look bad as administrators if kids appear to be "out of control." Rereading Jean Piaget (1969) reminds us that learning happens when people are in a state of disequilibrium. Teachers are learners when they implement new strategies and practices. Principals support teacher learning when they encourage risk taking in their schools. We celebrate innovations and professional stretching. We recognize that everyone, classroom teachers included, looks a bit disorganized when he or she tries something new.

When Jan, a teacher on Myna's staff, was attempting cooperative learning groups for the first time, Myna noticed Jan's frustration with the groups who were not "on task." Realizing that focusing on the disruptive students would jeopardize Jan's willingness to continue using cooperative strategies, Myna redirected Jan's attention to the students who were successful: "Why do you think those children were so engaged in the activity?" In answering that question, Jan focused on the positive aspects of the experience rather than the negative ones and thus received the encouragement she needed to continue using cooperative learning strategies.

Emphasizing strengths in the evaluation process rather than commenting negatively goes a long way toward establishing a safe climate. Recognizing strengths in one another allows us to rethink the term *weakness* and deal with the concept of *areas in which to grow.* As a concrete example of this idea, Bob crosses out the term ~~weaknesses~~ on the district-adopted teacher evaluation document and writes in *areas of growth.*

We believe that principals must continually take risks themselves. For a teaching staff to be on the cutting edge, to use innovative teaching/learning strategies that engage children's minds and hearts, principals must be willing to experiment with new ideas, to try new techniques and strategies in front of teachers and students.

When Lydia was transferred to Borton, she had little experience using shared reading strategies with her third graders. During his weekly read-alouds, Bob brought big books into the room and demonstrated how shared reading strategies support readers.

Empowerment to take risks safely makes teachers feel as if they own their teaching (and their learning) and generates a lot of excitement. We are passionate about our own learning and expect a similar passion in teachers, parents, and students.

Establish a Collaborative Environment

We want our teachers to be able to work in a collegial atmosphere. Everyone does not need to agree on everything, but everyone does need to treat others respectfully and hear their ideas as authentic. We therefore actively create and support an environment in which authentic voices and concerns can be raised and heard.

Collaboration can take place only when there are conscious efforts to provide the time and space for sustained dialogue. As principals we must be creative in building in quality time for our teachers to discuss and plan collaboratively:

- Schools that do not have to adhere to strict bus schedules can lengthen the school day by fifteen minutes four days a week and dismiss an hour early on the remaining day.
- Early dismissals for staff development can be built into district schedules.
- Teachers can work together while substitutes teach their classes.
- A principal (or a colleague) can lead several classrooms at a time in group experiences while the teachers of those classrooms collaborate.
- Office staff, curriculum support staff, and community experts can be recruited as guest teachers.

As teachers develop shared goals for children, they are rethinking and communicating their own philosophic stances. The process allows them to hear and understand the ideas of others. Sharing diverse views, strengths, and "multiple intelligences" (Gardner 1985) raises levels of thinking. "Meaty" issues like multiage classrooms, developmentally appropriate practices, and nonbiased curriculum can be wrestled with.

Everyone in the school community is watching us as administrators, assessing our responses. Wary teachers measure our words against our actions. We must recognize creativity and risk taking when it happens and allow for growth through approximation, especially in those who cannot handle a great deal of change in their professional lives. We have to be sensitive to the social and emotional needs of teachers whose personal and family lives are in turmoil. We must maintain high expectations and look for teachable moments when we can nudge, ask a leading question, or invite discussion rather than point out problems.

Confidentiality is a major factor in our efforts to establish a supportive and collegial environment. We speak privately with people about our concerns. Students are not embarrassed in front of their classmates or families, and staff members are never admonished in public. We work hard never to talk about others unless it is positive.

We cannot afford to "sit" on an issue raised by angry parents or staff members. We immediately arrange a meeting at which all parties are heard. This policy has a major impact on student discipline as well. Students are not just "punished"—we discuss the problem together and solve it so it won't happen again. (Discipline is discussed more fully in Chapter 8.)

No one can risk sharing new ideas in an atmosphere where staff members "tattle" on one another. We cannot have intermediate-grade teachers complaining to parents or their colleagues that the primary-grade teachers didn't do such and such, and so on down the line. If this happens, there have probably been too many grade-level meetings and not enough dialogue across grade levels. Everyone needs to be clear about the basic issues of trust inherent in a collegial environment.

A traditional "democratic" yea-or-nay vote often polarizes the community on issues that are not usually cut-and-dried. Consensus training shows us how to establish parameters in which everyone trusts his or her position will be heard, listens to one another more carefully, and comes to decisions everyone can live with. (Building a consensus is discussed in more detail in Chapter 6.)

Everyone has to agree that there will be disagreement at some times. Teachers and principals do not have to agree with one another to be respectful of others' feelings and ideas. This means when two teachers have a problem it is our job to remind them that they can work it out in private or that we will be happy to facilitate a formal mediation. The Warren staff met with a consultant who helped them develop a policy of "going to the source." When misunderstandings or disagreements arise, the people in question agree to problem-solve with each other instead of "talking it out" with everyone else.

Published programs that offer formal structures for assuring that every stakeholder has a voice are available from National Education Association affiliates and local mediation agencies. Borton staff (along with interested parents and students) went through formal conflict resolution training facilitated by the Arizona Education Association.

Focus Instruction on Learning

It doesn't matter how hard teachers "teach;" if the kids aren't learning, it doesn't count. The most up-to-date techniques and strategies in the world only count when students are learning. As constructivists, we see learning as happening when people (large and small) make connections with prior knowledge and experience. It is the teacher's job to assess the prior knowledge of individual students. We encourage our teachers to:

1. Kidwatch while they teach and reflect on those observations when they plan subsequent experiences.
2. Ask themselves why students behave or act in a certain manner in a particular context.
3. Reflect on the instructional implications of their curricular decisions.
4 Include kidwatching strategies when they evaluate student progress.
5. Use the community knowledge and support systems of the class as a social group to plan and orchestrate materials and create an environment in which all children can learn.

Promote a Professional and Scholarly Focus

To develop a teaching staff that is well read in both current and classic educational research and literature, we encourage our teachers to share interesting articles, become mentors to less experienced teachers, form study groups, and implement other professional development strategies. At Warren, the teachers and Myna hold a biweekly study group that addresses a wide variety of topics related to children's learning. This year, the Borton staff is conducting a mini-study of evaluation; five faculty meetings have been designated as opportunities for teachers to discuss their views about evaluation and their assessment techniques.

We also encourage our teachers to attend—and speak at—conferences. Teachers make expert decisions minute by minute in their classrooms, and it is important for them to share their craft with others and see themselves as experts. Planning and presenting in teams is a way to offer support to novice presenters. (Professional development processes are discussed in Chapter 6.)

Work Hard

A simple yet powerful concept! Good parenting, good teaching, and good "principaling," good anything, takes hard work. If principals expect 100 percent from parents, students, and staff, we need to demonstrate 150 percent. Others need to see that principals are not sitting back and waiting for work to come to them. They must see principals taking part in classrooms, meeting with parents, meeting with kids, out getting donations for the school. If our staffs are lethargic, we take a close look at ourselves.

Both of us provide a weekly announcement sheet (see Figures 4.1 and 4.2) to every staff member. All the important activities, field trips, assemblies, and changes in schedules are there. We also include our own schedule of administrative meetings, classroom interactions and observations, and meetings with kids, teachers, and parents. These are organized by the week to help teachers with their planning and to see how hard their principal works.

Make School a Place We Enjoy Returning to Each Day

Principals set the tone for fun in the school in what we say and how we respond to others. Schooling is hard work and everyone needs more fun at the workplace.

We believe that school should be the kind of place children want to return to each day too. The power of the learning community is in the excitement and the joy of learning. Students welcome their work when their class is one in which they enjoy spending time. We encourage laughter and try not to squelch spontaneity.

If we are not having fun, we will not want to come back each day; and if teachers and principals do not look forward to coming to school, it will reflect in job performance and interactions. Laughter is good medicine, and good-natured humor is generally appreciated in intense meetings or the faculty lounge.

The Borton staff does not encourage parties but does have schoolwide celebrations on afternoons preceding holidays. At that time the students, parents,

---

Borton Primary Magnet School Announcements

Week of August 22, 1994

Sunshine Room has pledge		Star Room has pledge next week
Lunch: 11:15 Romero/Rivera	11:20 Melendez/Olea	11:25 Bailey/Stritzel
11:55 Lomas/McCauley	12:00 Crowell/Walker	12:05 Lohse/Glenn

MONDAY 8/22/94

11:30	Child study meets in library
12:45	Bob meets with teaching assistants in Wildcat Room
2:00	Bob in Happy Face Room
4:00	Bob meets with PTA Board

TUESDAY 8/23/94

Bob on personal leave. Betty and Teri are designees.

WEDNESDAY 8/24/94

7:30	SBDM CORE meeting in library
8:45	Bob in the Fish Room
11:00	Bob in the Bear Room
2:00	Bob in the Zoo Room
2:40	FACULTY Meeting in the Zoo Room

THURSDAY 8/25/94

8:00	Bob meets with student teachers in Wildcat Room
11:00	Bob in Lion's Den
11:30	Bob in Sunshine Room
2:00	Interviewing for attendance clerk

FRIDAY 8/26/94

8:45	Bob in Kitty Kat Room
11:30	Bob in Star Room
12:45	Bob in Tree Room
1:15	Bob meets with Lois
3:30	Bob meets with Ms. Baison

STAFF:
• The most powerful P.R. of the year is when teachers take time to call each family the first week of school to share something positive and specific about the child. Please make sure you make a positive contact *before* you share any concerns that may arise.
• Monday, 8/22/94 at 12:45 P.M. I would like to meet with teaching assistants in the Wildcat Room. Bring notebooks and any desserts you would like to share.
• I will be out of the building on Tuesday, 8/23/94 on personal leave.
• Student council meeting Monday, 8/29, after pledge.
• I need a copy of everyone's schedule A.S.A.P.
• The CORE Committee has planned an all-staff meeting on Wednesday, 8/31, from 7:45-8:30. Please come to this important first meeting in the library.
• Thanks to everyone who shared goodies Friday. Let's do it again!

Figure 4.1 Borton staff announcements.

and staff come together to sing songs we all know. Teachers plan and perform readers theater productions such as "Too Much Noise," "The Jolly Postman," and "The Frog Prince Continues." These activities reflect the fun we have with books and with each other. Students and parents enjoy these celebrations as

---

Warren Times

May 6, 1994

TUESDAY Final PTA meeting of the year (7:00 P. M.).
FRIDAY   Pistor Middle School Chorus to perform for fourth and fifth grades (9:45 A. M.).
         All books returned to the library today.
         Last day computer lab is open.
         Myna to last principals' meeting of year (12:30 P. M.).

LOOKING AHEAD TO THE END...
MONDAY, May 16:   K–3 Grade Awards (9:15 A. M.)
                    Retirement party for Linda (7:00 P. M.)
TUESDAY, May 17:   RIF distribution
                    K–3 teachers meet (2:15 P. M.)
                    Mary Ellen to Lab Techs meeting all day
WEDNESDAY, May 18: Students' last day
                    Fifth Grade Promotion (9:30 A. M.)
                    K–4 Grade Awards (1:00 P. M.)
THURSDAY, May 19:   Teachers' last day
                    Cheers and Tears!* (11:30 A. M.)
TUESDAY, May 23:   Office closes (2:30 P. M.)

Congratulations Marie and Lesley for winning a $300 minigrant to publish a school news-letter next year.

*Cheers and Tears! The Social Committee is sponsoring a salad bar lunch and end-of-the-year gathering for everyone on the staff. A sign-up sheet for salad ingredients will be posted in the Staff Room. Social Committee funds will provide beverages and dessert.

Abby will be asking each employee for her/his summer address this week.

Open enrollment/change forms are available for medical and dental insurance, and pay-roll deduction rate sheets. If you want to make any changes, forms are available from Abby.

TEACHERS...
"Have a Cool Summer" post cards are in the office. If you are interested in including them in report cards or mailing them to students, you may pick up a set from the basket behind Abby's desk.

Figure 4.2 Warren staff announcements.

much as the staff. The laughter and the singing binds everyone together in ways that all the newsletters and all the announcements in the world can't.

"Joys and Sorrows" sessions at faculty and staff meetings allow us to share our high and/or low experiences for the week. Teachers also highlight successful classroom strategies at faculty meetings. These regular activities let us show that we care about one another and wish to hear the ups and downs of our colleagues' professional (and sometimes personal) experiences. In these ways we come to understand one another better and are better able to get along during hard times. A staff that laughs and cries together is more likely to work as a team.

Strengthen Communication Between School and Home

Effective schools have an inviting atmosphere where parents feel welcome no matter what their previous school experiences. Many homes have a comfortable family room where the family gathers for the daily routines and work of the home and a more formal living room set up for special occasions. In the living rooms of our houses we won't allow children (or adults) to be "messy." In our family rooms we can do messy activities and still "pick up for company."

Our schools and classrooms are set up like family rooms, not living rooms. There are times when productive and engaging learning environments are messy. (This is especially difficult for Myna, who has been accused by teachers of being excessively neat.) Hallways and classrooms reflect the authentic "work" of all the children. Their writing and artwork are displayed lovingly, respectfully, and aesthetically, and all children are represented, not just the best or most adultlike. It is clear to everyone entering our schools that we, as learning communities, celebrate the work of all children.

Building Community Through Shared School Goals

Even as we live our own beliefs and professional goals as principals, we negotiate schoolwide goals with our staff and parents. The power of schoolwide goals is not in formulating three, five, or seven objectives worded in a specific way, but rather in parents, teachers, staff, students, and the principal together discussing, negotiating, "hashing out," and agreeing on a set of common beliefs. A brainstorming process like the one we discussed in Chapter 6 is a powerful opportunity to establish a common focus and a shared language that is accepted and understood by everyone. The goals themselves are a filter through which ideas and activities are sifted.

Warren Elementary School's goals were written by the teachers and staff the year Myna became principal. Everyone together brainstormed a vision of the school. This vision was the framework from which later discussions, negotiations, and agreements established a set of shared school goals that are revisited each year.

After four years and a lot of staff turnover, Myna and the Warren teachers, staff, and parents decided the goals needed major revision. The teachers especially wanted to find a schematic that more accurately conveyed the holistic vision and nature of Warren's strategies for implementating learning and assessing accomplishments. Everyone felt that instead of the earlier linear format, a circular, interconnected, layered framework (see Figure 4.3) best exemplified the school goals and the processes that would help them succeed.

Borton Primary School's goals (see Figure 4.4) were established over the course of a year. The former principal (Bob was a kindergarten teacher at Borton at the time) worked with her faculty, staff, students, and parents at after-school and evening meetings to brainstorm the desirable attributes of a student leaving Borton after third grade. These lists were discussed, defended, and revised over the course of several months in various combinations: faculty and staff, parent and student, and faculty and parent groups. School goals were then developed from the attributes lists through a similar procedure.

Bob continues to revisit the original Borton goals each year with the faculty, staff, students, and parents. Over the years these goals have been modified, but they have not changed greatly.

Programs and Activities That Build Community

The concept of school as a community of learners guides our notions of literacy learning, our organizational practices, and our interactions with students, parents, and staff. Our conceptualization of how to build community has been refined by Ralph Peterson's *Life in a Crowded Place* (1992).

As whole language principals, we truly care about promoting and nurturing the concept of school as community. In addition to interacting with all community members every day and implementating shared goals, we continually introduce programs and practices that promote community and eliminate practices that encourage competition at the expense of community. Whole language principals continually seek ways to include rather than exclude.

Ambiance

We can't stress enough the power of the warmth established by the children's artwork in the hallways and the smiles that greet people when they come into the building and office. We want the ambiance of school to be that of a home, not a public building. Parents are invited into the classrooms. At Borton every classroom has a parent corner where parents can have a cup of coffee and stay as long as they like. At Warren a new parent room has been included in architectural plans for upcoming renovation. If parents want to help, there is always a stack of magazines from which pictures of animals, people, or food need to be cut out for later use. There are always pieces of children's artwork to be mounted, labeled, and displayed. And there are always children to read to, talk with, and listen to as they read their stories and share their research. We know that not every parent is suited or comfortable in the instructional role, but every parent is made welcome in the classroom and the school.

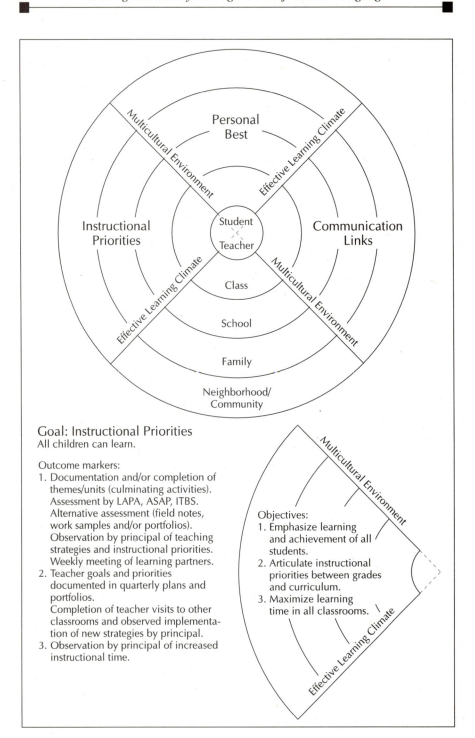

Goal: Instructional Priorities
All children can learn.

Outcome markers:
1. Documentation and/or completion of themes/units (culminating activities). Assessment by LAPA, ASAP, ITBS. Alternative assessment (field notes, work samples and/or portfolios). Observation by principal of teaching strategies and instructional priorities. Weekly meeting of learning partners.
2. Teacher goals and priorities documented in quarterly plans and portfolios.
   Completion of teacher visits to other classrooms and observed implementation of new strategies by principal.
3. Observation by principal of increased instructional time.

Objectives:
1. Emphasize learning and achievement of all students.
2. Articulate instructional priorities between grades and curriculum.
3. Maximize learning time in all classrooms.

Goal: Personal Best

Maintain an environment reflecting an expectation of excellence from students, teachers, support staff, parents, and administration; establish a school climate that fosters "personal best."

Outcome markers:
1. Assessment by multiple measures.
   Accomplishment of physical fitness program, Special Olympics, school spirit days.
2. Student work displayed all around the school.
   Clean environment noted in Client Satisfaction survey and by staff.
3. Student norms or rules visible in classrooms.
   Documentation of student behavior on behavior cards.
4. Record of meetings and accomplishments of student council.
   Observation of safety patrol.
   Successful evaluation of student teachers and cooperating teachers by university supervisor.
   Maintenance of staff norms and informal social activities at school.

Objectives:
1. Emphasize "personal best" (academic, social, physical, and emotional) and encourage intrinsic satisfaction for jobs well done.
2. Utilize the physical environment to reflect personal best.
3. Respect self, others, and property.
4. Promote an atmosphere that fosters collaboration and positive communication.

Multicultural Environment *Effective Learning Climate*

Goal: Communication Links

Strong school/family/community partnership that works together with mutual respect and appreciation of collective cultures of Warren community.

Outcome markers:
1. Open House.
   Newsletter from principal and PTA president.
   Teacher/principal initiate regular positive communication with parents from beginning of year.
   Partnership with PTA.
   Newsletters from each class.
   Room parents/telephone tree.
   Clear communication of school policies.
   Family workshops on whole language and mathematics.
2. Extend invitations to families and community to visit and participate at school.
   Recognize individuals and businesses for school participation.
3. Distribute RIF books to students.
   Build positive relationships back into the community (cultural events/food drives/clothing bank).
   REAP Sweep.

Effective Learning Climate *Multicultural Environment*

Objectives:
1. Maintain clear and open communication between school and home.
2. Encourage and recognize family and community contributions to the school.
3. "Give back" to the community around us.

Figure 4.3 Warren Elementary School goals.

Borton Primary Magnet School Goals

Borton's unique environment fosters the development of the whole child into a lover of learning. An integral component of the program is the involvement of parents in the education of their children. This provides opportunities for the learning process to be a shared responsibility involving children, home, and school. Opportunities are provided to foster the development of the higher-level thinking skills. These goals will serve all persons (students, parents, staff, volunteers, etc.) involved in Borton Primary Magnet School. They are intended to describe the school's overriding purposes and values and to provide focus for the development of the School Improvement Plan.

POSITIVE, ACCURATE SELF-CONCEPT: Adults will facilitate this goal by:
• Providing daily success experiences for all students.
• Assisting students to deal with success, criticism, and failure, to learn and build on experiences.
• Providing a multicultural/multilingual setting in which students value learning.
• Facilitating an awareness of the contributions and unique characteristics of students' cultures.
• Applying and sharing knowledge of equity through classroom activities and organizations.

RESPONSIBILITY AND SELF-DIRECTION: Adults will facilitate this goal by:
• Helping students to be responsible for their education and facilitating the education of others.
• Encouraging students toward self-discipline by awareness of the consequences of their own actions.
• Providing opportunities for students to grow in ability to make appropriate choices.

APPRECIATION AND RESPECT FOR OTHERS: Adults will facilitate this goal by:
• Providing ongoing opportunities for students to develop social interaction skills.
• Developing an atmosphere that nurtures trust building and open lines of communications.
• Demonstrating caring for others.
• Providing opportunities for students to recognize and value cultures other than their own.

SENSE OF THE AESTHETIC: Adults will facilitate this goal by:
• Creating an aesthetically pleasing environment and climate.
• Exposing students to the arts and fostering an appreciation of music, drama, art, dance, and literature.
• Deliberately modeling the appreciation of creations of others.

EXPRESSION OF CREATIVITY: Adults will facilitate this goal by:
• Promoting opportunities for children to compose with various media: paint, clay, language, etc.
• Supporting and providing time for creative efforts initiated by students.
• Allowing and valuing individual responses.
• Evaluating the creative processes so that students will recognize and value them.
• Developing students' awareness of their own environment and changes as they occur.

ACHIEVEMENT IN CURRICULUM AREAS: Adults will facilitate this goal by:
• Providing daily opportunities for students to read and be read to.
• Assisting students in communicating effectively through speaking, writing, and listening.
• Providing daily experiences in computation and problem solving.
• Providing students opportunities/strategies to learn basic skills through an integrated program.
• Recognizing and meeting the needs of individual learning styles.

ABILITY TO USE THE BODY EFFECTIVELY: Adults will facilitate this goal by:
• Modeling appropriate dress and encouraging students to dress appropriately for activities.
• Providing opportunities for students to develop locomotor (run, jump, hop), nonlocomotor (bend, twist, turn), and manipulative (dribble, catch, throw) skills.
• Providing opportunities for competency in managing the body in space around them.

COMPETENCE USING TOOLS AND APPARATUS: Adults will facilitate this goal by:
• Providing many experiences for using equipment that fosters growth of large and small muscles.
• Providing playground and P. E. equipment, classroom tools, machines, and manipulatives.
• Demonstrating and assisting in becoming computer literate.

Figure 4.4 Borton School goals.

Community Gatherings, Celebrations, and Sing-Alongs

Every morning after the bell has rung, the Borton community gathers in the school patio. There, each classroom in turn leads the Pledge of Allegiance ceremony for a week at a time. We sing a song as everyone gathers and we establish that everyone is present. (Singing focuses students' attention in a more positive way than shushing, finger snapping, and shouts of "Be quiet!" do.) After the initial song, the students who are holding the flag and who will lead us are introduced, and we then say the Pledge in unison. The class in charge then leads us in another song of their choice. Finally, the announcements are made and everyone is dismissed to begin classes. This is a special time, because it sets the tone for the day with a community gathered together, their voices raised in song, seeing one another's faces.

Every Tuesday afternoon groups of three or four classrooms at Borton gather for group sing-alongs. Sometimes they meet by grade level, but since there are so many multiage classrooms, these sing-alongs tend to be across grades as well. Here the students and staff learn new songs that often later become part of the morning Pledge ceremony. Kids gain experience by gathering in groups, singing parts and rounds, and working at beginning instrumentation with eighty others. It is a lovely sound we hear on those afternoons.

Community gathering is more informal and less frequent at Warren. New teachers who are used to community gatherings, like those held at Borton and some other schools in the district, often feel that Warren students need to spend more time together in order to build a greater sense of the whole. They believe that class pride and togetherness cannot take the place of a strong sense of school community. The Warren staff and students have therefore initiated a weekly schoolwide gathering on Monday mornings so that they can sing, say the Pledge of Allegiance, and start the week together.

Warren has other strong elements in its efforts to build community. Teachers get together biweekly in a study group to learn and problem-solve. Faculty and staff meetings encourage sharing in many forms. Classes learn together at least weekly as learning buddies or cross-age tutors. There are schoolwide assemblies and sing-alongs in addition to those held on Monday mornings.

We value being in schools where the students and staff know and care for each other, meet frequently, and enjoy learning together. We wouldn't want it to be any other way!

Schoolwide Themes

Schoolwide themes bring the staff and students together in learning and in sharing what they have learned. Both schools have employed schoolwide themes to enhance learning and to help build a sense of community.

A $15,000 DeWitt Wallace–Library Power Grant enabled Warren to undertake a two-year multicultural theme. The focus was on building self-esteem and on recognizing the many cultural, ethnic, and linguistic communities within the larger Warren community. At each grade level students learned about multicultural aspects of the history, aesthetics, and ecology of their environment. Areas of study included immigration, music, arts, human and animal homes, foods, successful graduates, and explorers of the southwestern United States.

The students demonstrated their learning in several ways. Each class produced—and published a guide to—a four-by-eight-foot art panel. Each panel was named and labeled in the four predominant languages of the area—English, Spanish, O'odham, and Yaqui. The panels were displayed in the school library, and the fourth graders, who typically study Arizona, served as library docents, giving tours of the art panels to other Warren students, visiting students from other schools, and adult friends and family members.

This community study culminated in an evening cultural fair that featured class exhibits, art projects, delicious food, entertainment, and narrated tours of the art panels. Yaqui dancers, Mexican folklorico dancers, and African drummers entertained. Students, parents, and grandparents prepared and sold foods from Mexico, the Philippines, Middle Eastern and African countries, and Arizona. Crafts and projects demonstrated the many cultures of the students and their families. Everyone had a wonderful time and learned about others from the Warren Elementary School community.

Borton took continents of the world (Asia, Africa, Central and South America) as their focus for several years, then storytelling, and later landmarks of the world. Each classroom demonstrated their learning through plays, displays, slide shows, and dioramas. The power of these theme studies became evident as people worked together, shared limited materials, and talked with and learned new ideas from one another.

When Borton students studied Asia, individual classes focused on topics such as tigers; pandas; the Olympic Games in Korea; family life in Japan; and the "Ring of Fire" in the Pacific Ocean. One class studied the caste system of India, comparing it with segregation in the southern United States, and then comparing the life and works of Mahatma Gandhi and Martin Luther King.

Most recently, a schoolwide ethnological study of the Borton community has been undertaken that will culminate in a book published for parents, the community, and other students in the district. The staff is looking forward to a variety of student experiences with organizing and evaluating data and writing across the curriculum.

Faculty and Staff Meetings

We have mentioned faculty meetings before as positive community builders and will discuss them in detail in Chapter 6. Rotating the meetings from classroom to classroom and asking the host teacher to facilitate the meeting, sharing successful teaching strategies, and raising "joys and sorrows," are powerful vehicles for promoting community among staff members.

Materials for Learning at Home

The concept of community exists beyond the four walls of our schools, because parents and other family members play such important roles in our schools. Sending learning materials home is an important way to maintain communication and support students' learning. Here are some successful examples of materials for home study generated by teachers from Warren and Borton.

Fine Art Backpacks.   Borton maintains thirteen fine art backpacks that students can check out for two-week periods. Students sign an agreement with parents about how the materials will be treated and used. Groups of students select the following items to go into their backpacks:

■   Cassette tapes of works by specific composers.
■   Miniature busts of the composers who wrote the music.
■   Portable cassette players with earphones or minispeakers.
■   Several books about fine arts or artistic and musical ideas.
■   Three or four minisculptures that represent other cultures from around the world.
■   Eight to ten miniart prints that have been cut out of magazines, calendars, or date books and laminated; the back has a caption about the artist or the print.
■   Plate stands for setting up the art prints as a museum display.
■   Current information from the Tucson Museum of Art and free bus passes to the museum for the family.

Ethnic Art Backpacks.   The ethnic art backpack program includes self-contained units about the local Native American, African American, Hispanic American and Asian American cultures. These backpacks contain all the items found in the fine arts backpacks plus:

■   Biographies of important people representing the ethnic group.
■   Traditional and contemporary music and art.
■   Stories from the culture.

This program has been instrumental in helping develop an understanding about the diversity of backgrounds in members of the school community.

Take-Home Computers.   When the school district provided Borton with a Macintosh computer laboratory, Borton staff set aside fourteen of their outdated Apple IIe's and IIGS's as computers for families to check out on a rotating schedule. Families can check out a computer and/or software for two weeks at a time if the parents will attend a five-hour training session on a Saturday, two school mornings, or two evenings. The training shows parents how to set up and repack the computer and how to use several pieces of software. The school will print any disks brought in by the parents. This program has been a very successful community builder and has given students who would not normally have the opportunity access to computers outside school.

Homework Packets.   In a school like Warren, which doesn't receive as much funding as a Magnet School like Borton, home-school communication looks more like it does in most schools. Weekly newsletters go home from most classes with information about what is happening in each class and the homework assigned. Several teachers have expanded this notion to include homework packets, which consist of fiction and nonfiction books along with discussion questions for students and their families in plastic bags or folders. Occasionally, tape recorders and cassettes of stories are included as well.

Book Bags.   Using State Dropout Prevention funds and other minigrants, some Warren teachers have put together book bags similar to the fine arts and ethnic arts backpacks used at Borton. The book bags were purchased at a discount store and all include one or more books on the same theme, materials for projects, and response logs.

Students are encouraged to read the books with the adults in their homes, and responses are encouraged from both the students and adults. There are book bags that focus on literature, social studies, science, art, and mathematics. An intermediate-grade book bag on homes includes:

- *A House Is a House for Me,* by Mary Ann Hoberman, illustrated by Betty Fraser (1978).
- *Fly Away Home,* by Eve Bunting, illustrated by Ronald Himler (1991).
- *Home: A Collaboration of Thirty Distinguished Authors and Illustrators of Children's Books to Aid the Homeless,* edited by Michael J. Rosen (1992).

Another intermediate-grade book bag, on the artist Paul Klee, includes:

- *Paul Klee,* written and illustrated by Mike Venezia (1991).
- Colored chalk, crayons, water colors, sponges, and paper.

A primary-grade mathematics book bag includes:

- *Henry and Mudge,* by Cynthia Rylant, illustrated by Sucie Stevenson (1987).
- *John Patrick Norman McHennessy: The Boy Who Was Always Late,* by John Burningham (1987).
- *Ruby the Copycat,* by Peggy Rathmann (1991).
- Mathematics problems and a calculator.
- Discussion questions on making new friends.

Another primary-grade book bag, this one focusing on the rain forest, includes:

- *Amazon Boy,* written and illustrated by Ted Lewin (1993).
- *The Great Kapok Tree,* by Lynne Cherry (1990).
- The "Crazy Rain Forest" game.

Celebrations

Birthdays are powerful rites of passage for children, and they are celebrated in some manner by most cultural groups attending our schools. We like to acknowledge birthdays and to celebrate the diversity of our communities in our classrooms and at school functions. Individual classrooms in both schools celebrate student birthdays, and Borton students, staff, and parents acknowledge staff member birthdays at the morning gatherings. Everyone sings "Happy Birthday" and "Las Mañanitas," a Mexican folksong traditionally sung at family birthdays in the Southwest. Celebration in two languages reminds the community of the cultural heritage shared by many of the children and shows a language other than English being used in an authentic context.

At Warren, where several teachers have celebrated landmark birthdays over the past few years, classes have begun serenading adults on their birthdays. Students and teachers develop a sense of sharing when they work "secretly" as peers to plan a celebration.

Whole language classrooms and schools balance traditional European American celebrations of Christmas and Easter by focusing on how a variety of cultures celebrate holidays. In December, Kawanza, Hanukkah, Las Posadas, and the Epiphany are discussed in the context of the multicultural curriculum, and the often overwhelming images and activities focusing on Santa and his reindeer are downplayed.

In our schools, with their large Hispanic population, el día de los muertes is highlighted as much as a traditional Halloween. Native American celebrations like powwows and other traditional dances are acknowledged as well. Whole language principals recognize that they need to ensure that the contributions and traditions of all ethnic and cultural groups within the school community are acknowledged and celebrated. It is equally important to expand the multicultural focus of the community beyond the boundaries of its own constituency. It is impossible to "celebrate" all the cultural groups equally, but it is possible to learn about other cultures through their traditions and make connections with one's own experiences. In doing so, the perspective of the community is broadened and strengthened.

Student-of-the-Week

Many classrooms at Borton and Warren maintain a child-of-the-week program in some form. The power of programs that highlight the strengths and special contributions of all children in the classroom is remarkable. Every student is highlighted in photographs, artifacts (a favorite toy, baby clothes, etc.), and personal recollections by family members visiting the classroom. Students are congratulated by their peers verbally or in writing. And if a classmate is a Spanish speaker, English speakers must find a bilingual student to interpret or translate.

As principals, we acknowledge the contributions of students, parents, and staff members in a variety of ways—letters, notes, newsletters, posters, announcements. We always have to be wary however not to fall into the trap of rewarding only academic efforts. Every student deserves to be recognized for her or his authentic contributions and strengths. We believe that schoolwide programs like student-of-the month are not nearly as powerful as more regular and widespread recognition, because not every student can possibly be recognized.

Schoolwide Postal System

Writing is an important way to communicate, and students use writing for authentic purposes when they write letters. Schoolwide postal systems are an important means of building community through literacy.

Both our schools have postal systems. Borton's is operated by a bilingual second-third combination classroom. The PTA provides a mailbox for every classroom and the office. Every classroom has a logo that identifies that classroom, so very young students can draw a picture of the class logo rather than write out the classroom name. Everyone in the school can write to everyone else. Adults are bound by the norm—if you receive a letter, you must write a letter in return.

Bob uses the postal system to write letters of encouragement and letters of thank-you. He also follows up on discipline concerns by asking students how things are going.

Warren's postal system is sponsored by the Student Council and is especially active during special times of the year. During the winter holiday season and on Valentine's Day, it's in full swing. Students write messages to children in other classes and adults in the building. All the adults answer the letters they receive. It is expected that "nice words" only will be written, and in the vast majority of instances this holds true. Children write a full address and return address on each envelope, so letter-writing conventions are learned in context.

Whenever a class writes books, displays art or written work in the hallways, or walks exceptionally carefully to the cafeteria, Myna writes that class a note. Students also write her about school problems or to thank her for reading to their class. This important communication helps students see the principal as a writer and someone who likes them and supports their learning.

Teachers regularly have students write to friends and family outside school and to pen pals from other areas of the United States. Students write letters asking for information and taking care of business transactions. These student letters are sent to their real audiences via the district mail service.

In our whole language schools we, as principals, set the climate for learning. We "walk the talk," demonstrating our view that learning occurs in natural settings in response to authentic purposes. We are learners, and we encourage everyone in the school to view themselves as learners too.

Dear Dr. Matlin,

I appreciate the way you try to build peace in our school. How many fights does it take to get suspended? If I got kicked out of 3 schools could I go to school anymore? Has anybody from Warren been kicked out of school, if so how many? How long have you been a principal? Please write back soon, if you can.

Sincerely,

Daniel

CHAPTER
FIVE

What Does Discipline Look Like in a Whole Language School?

Discipline and a Positive Climate for Learning

Most students who care about their learning and are working cooperatively don't require disciplinary measures. That's why the principal's first focus of time and energy needs to be on curriculum and classroom organization. An effective discipline program emerges from a strong community of learners and a student-centered, content-rich curriculum. If the content is integrated and engaging and the community supportive, then the work of discipline is halfway done.

An Adlerian interactive model (Dreikers and Soltz 1964) describes the discipline programs at both our schools. All behavior is recognized as purposeful, with children and adults held accountable for their own actions. We don't ever discount the value of the individual. We may not agree with a child's (or an adult's) actions, but we show that we care about the person.

An established resource for this type of model is Dreikers and Soltz's *Children: The Challenge* (1964). The school environment is structured so that students make deliberate decisions pertaining to their learning and behavior. Children and adults alike are expected to follow accepted societal demands of general courtesy and to accept responsibility for their own behavior. Consequences are logical and tied to the infraction, not arbitrary and unproductive. Behavior issues are viewed as learning opportunities.

As principals and leaders, we strongly believe that collaborative communities and a comfortable emotional climate cannot be established and maintained if school discipline is oppressive, retributive, and unwieldy. The best discipline program is proactive and consistent with the agreed-on schoolwide goals. Using a districtwide model, each of our communities has built a discipline plan that grows out of our school goals and expectations. The discipline policies at our schools are revisited every few years and have sustained some revision (Warren will review and revise its policy this coming school year), but the essence of the spirit of community still remains.

The Borton community works together continuously each year to identify the components of a positive social and emotional climate. Parents and teachers agree that a positive climate for learning reflects caring, friendliness, trust, decisiveness, responsibility, consistency, and warmth. In day-to-day interactions, everyone strives to maintain a climate that continually reflects these values and adults are expected to demonstrate these qualities.

Three overall schoolwide goals for students at Borton provided a foundation for parents and staff to create the school discipline policy. These goals were brainstormed, revised, and simplified over a year's time by a committee of students, parents, and staff. Each child at Borton will:

- Build a positive and accurate self-concept.
- Take responsibility and exhibit self-direction.
- Demonstrate appreciation and respect for others.

Warren's behavioral goals, which were developed and agreed on by the teaching staff, are similar to Borton's: a safe and orderly learning environment will be established by:

- Building students' self-esteem.
- Encouraging respect for self, other students, adults, and property.
- Using positive problem-solving techniques.
- Promoting safety for all.

Positive and Accurate Self-Concept/Self-Esteem

For children to view themselves as lifelong learners, it is important that all children feel some success during each school day. Bob reminds faculty and staff members that it is their primary responsibility to make sure that every student looks and feels smart every day. The curriculum must be sufficiently broad and be adaptable to a variety of learning styles and structures to ensure that students learn through successes, not from repeated failures. Teachers, through ongoing assessment and kidwatching, plan and facilitate experiences that help children learn to deal with success, criticism, and even failure.

Students should own their learning and feel they belong in their school. Some ways to achieve this are for students to display their work; self-assess their learning; have choices in what they study, read, and write; and take part in developing classroom norms.

Teachers at our schools continually apply their knowledge of equity through their curriculums, classroom activities, and organization. Role models representing the gender, ethnicity, and linguistic diversity of the students are provided through a variety of media and community outreach resources. In thematic studies, teachers very deliberately bring in guest experts that represent a variety of ethnic groups and highlight men and women in a range of roles.

The curriculum is daily infused with literature that reflects the contributions and unique characteristics of students' cultures. It is important for teachers to identify authors and illustrators that represent the ethnic and cultural diversity of the community. These books are concrete examples of the contributions of people from many cultures. Our librarians work with teachers in choosing read-alouds and books for discussion. Teachers at Borton have created a special card catalogue file in which the library fiction collection has been identified according to ethnic origin of the author, illustrator, and major characters. Second-language issues are given similar attention.

Responsibility and Self-Direction/ Using Positive Problem-Solving Techniques

We want students to be responsible for taking ownership of their own learning and schooling and facilitating the education of others. Students have many opportunities to make choices and reflect on the appropriateness of those choices. They learn that their actions have consequences.

We expect teachers to provide opportunities for students to explore materials and themes in general and then tap into students' important questions to negotiate a curriculum that is engaging and problem-centered. Students work cooperatively on many projects and hold one another accountable for the contributions and success of the group. Self-evaluations routinely include questions about what students have learned and what their most important contributions to the group have been.

When students are not getting along they are responsible for reflecting on those contexts in which they are able to work collaboratively and are expected to make a plan they can follow when future conflicts arise. Students never return to a classroom or other group activity from which they have been removed without a plan for what can be done differently next time. They are always expected to share their plan with the teacher or other offended party.

Appreciation and Respect for Self, Other Students, Adults, and Property

There are ongoing opportunities for students to develop social interaction strategies in a variety of settings—on the playground, during group games, as part of individual and small-group projects, in conferences. Our students are trained in conflict resolution techniques and know the consequences of not getting along. This deliberate focus on accepting individual feelings and understanding the points of view of others is an important facet of any responsible member of society.

The school culture provides many opportunities for students to recognize and value cultures and languages other than their own. Students who can communicate in two languages are bilingual role models. Communication requires trust and understanding. In a multilingual environment communication must be a daily goal. The adults also communicate in two languages. Teachers and staff members risk speaking in a second language. Parents and students who speak a second language are complimented so others can see that learning a second and third language is important to becoming a lifelong learner.

Promoting Safety for All

There must be an atmosphere that nurtures trust and opens lines of communication. Caring for others and for property must be demonstrated. Students are always asked to verbalize how they can keep themselves, others, and property safe. For learning to occur, students and adults must feel safe at school and on the way to and from school. There must be a shared expectation that school is a place for learning, not just for controlling students.

An environment in which everyone has positive self-esteem, appreciates and respects others, and uses self-directed problem-solving strategies is our goal. As our students come and go, we continually revisit norms and consequences for fighting and using racially biased language; we have occasionally had to deal with weapons (particularly knives) in school.

It often surprises students and parents to learn that Arizona law holds the principal responsible for "discipline" to and from school—from door to door. Our challenge as principals is not to be police officers looking over the shoulders of all our students from the moment they leave their homes each morning; rather, it is to be leaders who are responsible for creating and sustaining an expectation that school is a worthwhile place for students to spend their time and energies. We must assure the community that the school norms will be adhered to—not to control student behavior, but to provide students with the freedom from fear and reprisal they need to explore their world and learn how to learn.

Establishing Expectations for Behavior

Discipline policies in our district (and we imagine everywhere), whether they are called goals, rules, standards, or norms, establish expectations for behavior. They describe acceptable behavior at school. At Warren, schoolwide standards are specific and reflect the combined expectations of the staff. They are meant to foster an environment that encourages learning and the desire to achieve. One danger of writing these specifics is that children and adults always find at least one detail you did not think of including. For the most part the standards specifically describe accepted, positive behaviors (though several negatives slipped in). They are worded in positive contexts because it doesn't help people to know what not to do, but it does help people to know what to do.

1. Students use effective problem-solving strategies in conflict situations. There is no fighting at school, on school grounds, or when traveling to or from school.
2. Students walk in the halls, classrooms, cafeteria, and parking areas.
3. Students keep rocks, sand, dirt, or other objects on the ground.
4. All adults in the building are shown respect and their directions are followed.
5. Students use language appropriate to school. Foul or obscene language, ethnic slurs, or other derogatory comments are not permitted.
6. Students stay at school and on school grounds after they arrive in the morning until they are dismissed at the end of the school day, unless checked out by a parent or guardian.
7. Students remove outdoor clothes when in the building in order to assume a positive stance for learning. (This is not one of the most popular rules, because some teachers, who have also agreed to follow the practice, think that on "bad hair days" the students should be allowed to wear hats inside; but most of us think the stance for learning needs to be maintained.)
8. Students eat in the cafeteria and dispose of litter properly.
9. Gum is not chewed at school.
10. Toys, sports equipment, skateboards, or other items that cause disruption of learning and/or harm remain at home.

The Borton staff believes that less is more and over the years has developed three simple guidelines for their primary school. The three main norms for Borton are:

1. You only do things that keep yourself safe.
2. You only do things that keep others safe.
3. You only do things that keep property safe.

Whenever there is a problem, Bob asks the kids, "Was that keeping you safe? Was it keeping other people safe? Was it keeping property safe?" He believes that these three questions cover most of the problems that arise at Borton. Sometimes kids write letters of apology, and sometimes they are invited to a lunch meeting with Bob and other concerned individuals. Sometimes they are asked if they are willing to have the problem mediated by trained student mediators. But the discussion always returns to the original norms.

Responsibilities and Consequences

The discipline policy at Borton spells out the responsibilities adults and children have for maintaining a safe community for learning. Adults have the responsibility to:

- Speak calmly and respectfully at all times.
- Be available to talk to students.
- Take students to their teacher, principal or designee, or another applicable adult.
- Follow up and be consistent.
- Maintain high standards for behavior.
- Set and explain parameters collaboratively.

Students are expected to:

- Talk over problems.
- Use positive language.
- Talk with an adult or student mediator.
- Treat others with respect at all times.

In Warren's more formal policy, consequences for negative behavior are spelled out for each step of progressive discipline. Teachers keep "discipline cards" noting special events of positive and negative behavior. Myna encourages teachers to contact parents early with examples of positive behavior and to document these positive contacts. Teachers also use the cards to document the procedures for student and parent contact in order to share responsibility for improving negative behavior. Here are Warren's progressive discipline steps:

1. A teacher/student conference is held to define the problem and establish the means for developing appropriate changes in behavior.
2. Parents are informed by telephone of problems and consequences.
3. Parents are informed in writing and are requested to continue working cooperatively with the student and teacher to implement positive change.
4. A parent/teacher/student conference is held to discuss solutions and a joint plan for improved behavior.

5. A parent/student/teacher/principal conference is held to develop a written plan for improvement.

The district Student Code of Conduct is followed in cases of severe misconduct, and Myna becomes involved immediately.

Involving Parents

By making positive connections with families before there are problems, we can make future meetings less threatening. Just as we expect teachers to contact parents during the first week of school to begin establishing positive rapport, we too begin to make positive contacts with parents as soon as possible. We try never to raise a concern unless we have first shared some positive anecdote or observation with parents.

We believe that parents must be collaborators with the school staff if any real change in students' behavior is to occur. First, parents need to know that teachers and the principal care about their children as individuals, and to that end principals must build trust and establish an atmosphere of mutual respect and support. This requires continual communication from both directions—home and school. True dialogue can never take place when either party is angry, defensive, or posturing.

We also attempt to focus consistently on school goals and norms, and implement our Adlerian philosophy when meeting with parents of obstreperous children. The child is not bad but is behaving in an unacceptable manner. Parents are informed and expected to assist in creating a plan that everyone involved can unequivocally support.

Establishing Classroom Norms

Within the first hour of the first day, classroom teachers are expected to:

1. Show kids where to go to the toilet.
2. Show kids where to throw up.
3. Discuss how to get along together as a family and post a rough draft of the classroom norms.

By the end of the second day, we expect every classroom to have posted a final copy of classroom norms to which the teacher, kids, substitutes, and other visitors can refer. We both like the term *norms* rather than *rules* because it implies a social necessity to adhere to general standards for the benefit of the group. Rules generally are imposed from above. Norms imply a social responsibility to the group and consistently place the responsibility for the behavior back on the individual. They need to be worded positively so that everyone will know what *to do* rather than what *not to do*. "Why are you choosing to interrupt your friend when it's her turn to talk?"

Substitutes are asked to refer to the norms left in every plan book at Borton, included in special substitute folders at Warren, and posted at both schools. They go over the norms with the students at the beginning of the day and refer to them when there are problems—thus distancing an adult who may not know the students well from a possible confrontation.

One resource for establishing classroom norms that Warren teachers have found helpful is the ASCD book *Discipline with Dignity,* by Curwin and Mendler (1988). This book describes procedures and examples for establishing class norms and expectations for positive behavior. It illustrates how to establish consequences in order to build a community of learners and promotes individual commitment for positive discipline.

Role of the Whole Language Principal

Going to the principal's office shouldn't be a scary experience. It should be a pleasure for students to visit and talk with the principal. We make a point to have students visit the office in small groups and individually. The principal's office is often used by the student mediators for mediation. Bob has on occasion even moved all his furniture against the wall and asked a whole classroom in for a read-aloud or storytelling. New students are invited to the office to meet Myna and the office staff as part of their introduction to Warren.

It is not the principal's job to maintain a jail for kids and be the resident warden. The purpose of a positive discipline climate isn't to catch students being bad—it's to catch kids being good. It's our job to help students learn about getting along together.

A principal's office is much like a teacher's classroom. It should reflect our interests and personality and be comfortable to spend time in. We refuse to turn our offices into prisons just because students need to be removed from classrooms. Bob has a small desk facing a blank part of one wall for kids who need a time-out place to concentrate on their work—but he uses it only when alternatives have had no effect. Myna also has a desk in a small conference room next to her office, a quiet area for reflection and catching up when it cannot be accomplished in the child's classroom or that of the buddy teacher. Each teacher at Warren has a buddy teacher who has agreed ahead of time (usually at the beginning of the year) to have students visit his or her room when it is not possible for them to work in their own room.

We both maintain a portion of our professional book and journal collection in our offices. We feel that it is important for both students and adults to see us as lovers of books and knowledgeable about professional materials. Of course our books can be checked out by students, staff, and parents. Myna's collection of children's books (about seventy-five), teddy bears, and toy trains provides discussion points and activities for "getting children's minds off their problems." Bob has about five hundred children's books at school that rotate in and out of his home collection. He also maintains a collection of stuffed toys that correspond to his favorite books (Paddington from *A Bear Called Paddington,* by Michael Bond [1960], the eponymous hero of *Curious George,* by H. A. Rey [1973], Lyle the crocodile from *The House on East Eighty-Eighth Street,* by Bernard Waber [1973], Peter from *Peter Rabbit,* by Beatrix Potter [1986], Max from *Where the Wild Things Are,* by Maurice Sendak [1963], *Strega Nona,* by Tomie de Paola [1975], and the cat from *The Cat in the Hat,* by Dr. Seuss [1957], to name only a few). The stuffed characters may be used by children to calm down, to demonstrate what happened in an altercation, or to convey how they feel if emotions are high.

Books and Discipline

Books are powerful resources for learning in both academic and social settings and are essential to the curriculum at Warren and Borton. Just as we expect teachers to read books that will help students deal with classroom issues, we also read books in classrooms that help work through problems that come up in the school. We choose specific books and poetry that deal with feelings, being connected to others, handling emotions, and problem solving in the classrooms.

Bob maintains a schedule of twenty to thirty minutes in each classroom every week. It's his way of keeping tabs on the pulse of the school and the easiest way for all the kids and adults to see him in the role of a teacher, a learner, and a problem solver. Myna is more apt to read to classes when invited or when dealing with specific problems.

Books we have had a great deal of success with include:

- *Alexander and the Terrible, Horrible, No Good, Very Bad Day,* by Judith Viorst (1972). A wonderful book that leads to discussion on alternative ways to handle anger other than hitting or name-calling.
- *Best Friends,* by Steven Kellogg (1990). A story about friends who have a falling-out and then make up.
- *People,* by Peter Spier (1980). A great book to spark discussion on diversity and the coming together of people who are different in skin color, language, and customs but similar in many other ways.
- *The Principal's New Clothes,* by Stephanie Calmenson (1989). A rewrite of the *Emperor's New Clothes.* You need to be willing to laugh at yourself,

but the kids love it! It involves issues of using one's head, not trying to impress others just to go along with the crowd, and telling the truth.

- *Where the Wild Things Are,* by Maurice Sendak (1963). This story demonstrates that there is a time and a place for running and yelling. It also prompts a wonderful discussion on forgiveness and the importance of being included.
- *Friends,* by Henrich Heine (1986), helps children deal with the issue of what best friends can do together and what they can't do together. Everyone sometimes needs time apart no matter how close they are.

Writing and Discipline

Writing is never used as a punishment (having kids write, "I will not throw rocks" over and over, for example). The message there is that writing is hard, we know it's hard and not supposed to be fun, so we're going to make you do it for a punishment. Writing "to get even" or as punishment is not consistent with the environment we want to create. However, we do ask students to write as a consequence of their behavior. They write letters of apology to custodians for stuffing paper towels down a toilet and to their parents to tell them how they used the paper towels. They write letters of apology to playground monitors for using bad language and to their parents to let them know they chose that language and what language they will choose in future. They write letters of apology to a friend for throwing a rock at her, to the parents of the child who was hit, and to their own parents explaining what has happened in case there is a phone call from the other child's parents.

We also have children write contractual agreements about what they are willing to do when similar situations arise in the future. We write to students several days or a week after an altercation to let the students know that we are on top of the situation and care about how they are feeling. Myna drops student and class messages in teachers' mail boxes. The schoolwide postal system at Borton is especially effective for corresponding with individual students and keeping tabs on their emotional barometer.

CASE STUDIES

The Substitute

A second-grade class was not behaving for their substitute teacher. The substitute had been at the school before and knew that he would get support from Myna, so he sent for her. She talked to the class, stressing how

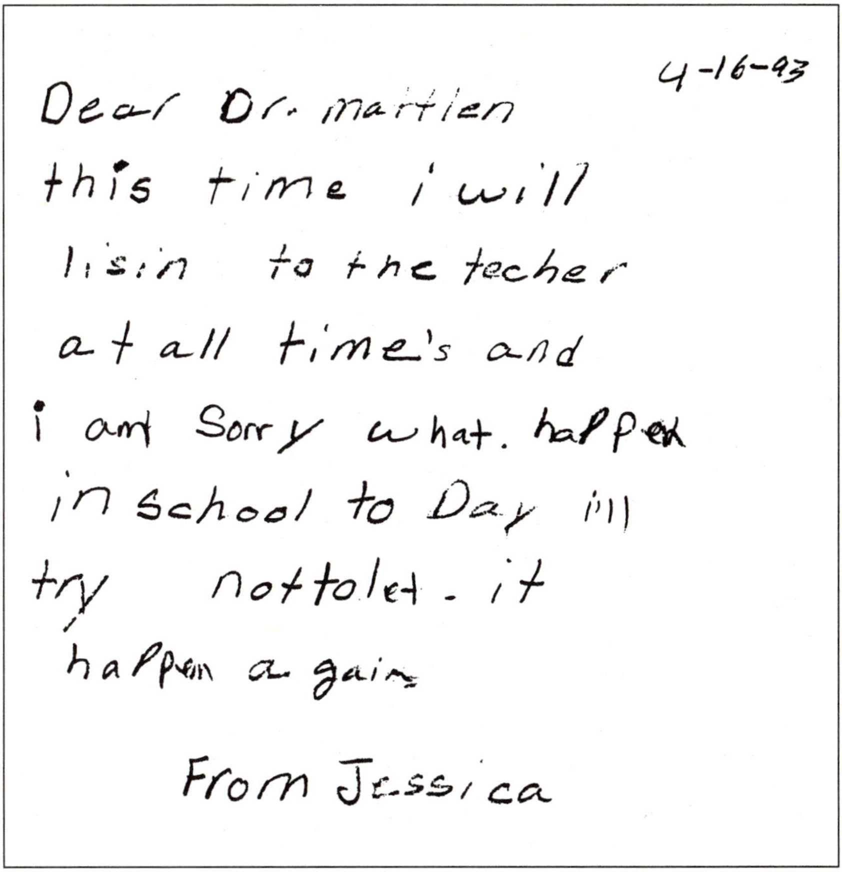

> Dear Dr. martien   4-16-93
>
> this time i will
>
> lisin   to the techer
>
> at all time's and
>
> i am Sorry what. happen
>
> in school to Day i'll
>
> try   nottolet. it
>
> happen a gain
>
>   From Jessica

Figure 5.1

much work she had to do and how the poor behavior of the class was keeping her from it. Mr. Johnson, the substitute, then had the class write letters of apology for interrupting the principal's work and for misbehaving (see Figure 5.1).

The next time the classroom teacher knew she would be out, she had the second graders write to their families to tell them how they would behave for the substitute while the teacher was away (see Figure 5.2). They all promised good behavior and for the most part lived up to their promises.

> dear mom,
> Ms. HOOD is not going to be here we will be with a another teacher for 2 days I will behave good
> Travis

Figure 5.2

Kids Hurting Kids

One morning when Bob was out of the building, Andrew poked Richard in the neck with a paper clip wire during journal time in kindergarten. The teacher was the principal designee that day and made sure that Andrew escorted Richard to the nurse's office to stay with him until everyone was certain Richard was okay.

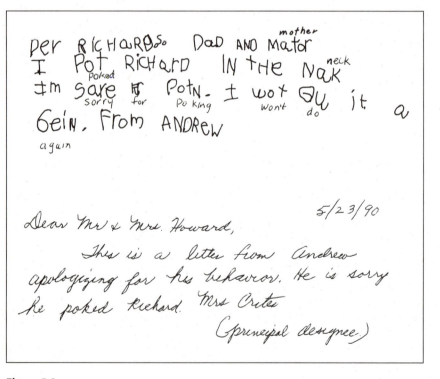

Figure 5.3a

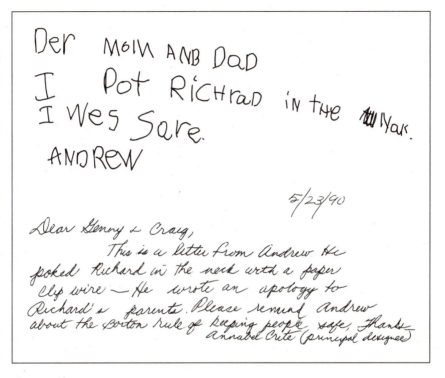

Der MoIM ANB DaD
I Pot RiCHraD iN tHe NYak.
I Wes Sare.
ANDReW

5/23/90

Dear Jenny & Craig,
    This is a letter from Andrew He
poked Richard in the neck with a paper
clip wire — He wrote an apology to
Richard's parents. Please remind Andrew
about the Boston rule of keeping people safe, Thanks
                        Annabel Crite (principal designee)

Figure 5.3b

Andrew was then asked to write a letter to Richard's parents explaining why Richard was coming home with a Band-Aid on his neck. Andrew also needed to write a letter to his own parents to let them know why Richard's parents could be calling (the families knew each other). Afterward, the teacher wrote a brief explanation on the bottom of Andrew's notes to both sets of parents (see Figures 5.3a and 5.3b).

Fighting

The fourth graders were building forts out in the "desert" area of the Warren playground and several refused to allow Stanton to play in their fort. A fight started when the ostracized boy entered the fort without permission. After breaking up the fight, a playground monitor brought the boys into the office to meet with Myna, after first taking Carlos to the health office for repairs. The boys wrote letters explaining to their moms and dads why the principal would be contacting them (see Figures 5.4a and 5.4b).

Dear mom I got in To
a fite. I was going in To
a fort win Andy send no.
sowe I went any wasy
Thin Corlos kint me in
The Hed - I got mad So
I theow Him on a rock

Stanton

Figure 5.4a

Dear Mom,

I got in a fight at
school and I got in trouble,
because we were playing in
the desert and stanton a friend
wanted to go where me and
Andy where going so I told him
not to go in the desert and I kick
him in the face and he pushed
me and threw me to the ground
and I hit a Rock on my
head and I had to go to
the nurse's office and the princ
ipal's office.

from Carlos

Figure 5.4b

Chaos in the Bathroom

Twelve first-grade boys ran excitedly into the boys' bathroom to prepare for the first field trip of the year. A parent helper did not anticipate the speed or exuberance of six-year-olds and the resulting commotion caught Bob's attention. He arrived amid a flurry of flying paper towels, shoving, and screaming. After a discussion of appropriate bathroom behavior, the boys cleaned up their mess and were escorted back to their classroom for the field trip. They were reminded however that they would need to meet with the principal immediately upon their return to make a plan to ensure that such an occurrence would never happen again.

After the field trip, they met in Bob's office and decided to put up a sign explaining the rules for using bathrooms at school. They appointed Tom as scribe and listed all the possible problems that had ever been discussed by the principal (see Figure 5.5). Afterward the list was edited, each boy recopied it, and the signs were placed in every bathroom in the school (including adult restrooms).

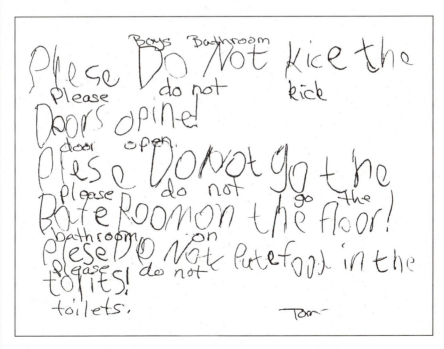

Figure 5.5

Our main problem is when we are outside at lunch and at recess. We have problems when we play rough.
What we need to do:

1. be friends and play with each other
2. not play rough
3. when we are mad we will talk it out first or go to Ms Arechederra or Mr. Wortman

If we have problems that continue we can;
1. lose lunch and recess time
2. write a letter to the other person's family
Keith 3. have a parent come in

GLEN

Bob Wortman

Figure 5.6

The Contract

Keith and Glen were not getting along on the playground during lunchtime. They had already been given time-out several times during previous days for punching each other. They had agreed to play in different areas of the play-ground, but always gravitated back to one another. When the monitors referred them to the principal for fighting, Bob asked them to eat together in his office the next day so they could come up with a plan that would keep everyone safe. Figure 5.6 is a copy of the contract they made with Bob. It was signed and copies given to the monitors, their classroom teachers, and their parents. Bob taped one above his desk to remind him in case they had to be referred to him again.

Dear Dr. Matlin,

I would like you to come this Friday for an art project at 1:15, but if you can't make it we have art every afternoon.

Sincerely
Eric

Mrs. Kahn's class

Professional Development and Decision Making

Principals' decisions about discipline and evaluation and about how they will interact with community, parents, staff, and students reflect their educational beliefs. We practice our whole language philosophy of constructing meaning through social interactions in the many administrative functions we perform. In fact, we attempt to demonstrate our philosophies in everything we do and say. We use our understanding of empowerment, learning, and learning communities to focus on school goals in the daily routines of planning, organizing, hiring, scheduling, working with staff, and overseeing professional development. Professional development and decision making are built into everything we do. By living our beliefs we provide the best professional development possible for our teachers, staff, students, and community—learning by doing.

The research literature on effecting school change indicates that no change has a realistic chance of succeeding unless all participants are thoroughly involved in the process, are able to identify and address problems as they see them, and can make the change their own (Fullan and Pomfret 1977; Lester and Onore 1990). We concur: change, learning, and decision making are integral parts of who we are and what we do each day. Although we see professional development and decision making as inherently overlapping concepts, we discuss each separately for convenience.

Professional Development

Professional development is at the heart of whole language as a philosophy and belief system. True teaching and learning is the work of informed practitioners. We recognize that professional growth occurs in a variety of formal and informal contexts and that Cambourne's conditions for learning (1988) are integral to effective professional development. We put his principles to use by integrating the following components into our professional development planning:

- Demonstration.
- Collaboration.
- Teacher visitation.
- Consultants.
- Teacher study groups.
- Principal study groups.

Demonstration

As instructional leaders we schedule time to be in classrooms demonstrating lessons and/or working collaboratively with teachers in order to live our important instructional leadership role. We strongly believe principals need to demonstrate their passion for learning and teaching within the context of their curricular strengths. Students, teachers, and parents need to see us in classroom instructional settings in order to respect our instructional suggestions as authentic. Bob loves to read and write with children and goes into classrooms as often as possible to read books that deal with classroom or schoolwide issues to children and to demonstrate minilessons. Myna team teaches with teachers in literature study groups. Principals who love mathematics should use problem-solving strategies with students, and those who love science should perform experiments with students. Students learn from these interactions, and so do principals and teachers.

Sometimes when we have set aside time to demonstrate a lesson, an emergency will arise—an angry parent or disruptive child will need attention—and we rush away leaving a classroom teacher with thirty children and an empty time slot. Good teachers handle the situation with seeming ease, but it is still a problem. Bob deals with this dilemma by scheduling himself to read in all the classrooms on a regular weekly schedule. That way, if an emergency arises, he leaves the book for the teacher to read or the teacher chooses another book.

Collaboration

Teacher leadership and collaboration is an important goal for both of us. Grade-level and cross-grade-level planning are equally effective for establishing collaboration, particularly as the benefits of multiage classrooms are becoming recognized (Kasten and Clarke 1993). Teachers select for themselves specific areas in which they are interested and/or would like a little help. They establish the curriculum areas, problems, tasks, or ideas to be discussed and work together to plan and teach.

We often use existing resources to support the teaching staff's cooperative planning and curriculum meetings. We sometimes take over classrooms ourselves to allow teachers to plan or organize activities that will benefit the whole school. We give priority to a group of teachers who would like to collaborate on a project together. We can bring in a speaker or get hold of a movie that ties into classroom themes and then supervise the students during the speech or while the movie is shown. Bob checked out several movies on safety issues to show students from five classes while their teachers planned a schoolwide theme on sanctuary.

Teachers and principals also need time and opportunities to work with all members of the school community. Faculty and schoolwide staff meetings can be configured to promote interaction, collaboration, and planning. Parents and community members can be invited to join school committees and come to meetings.

Teacher Visitation

As we discuss in Chapter 4, an important aspect of teachers' learning together is giving them time to visit other classrooms so they can observe teaching and learning in a variety of settings. This has proven to be an excellent way to develop collegiality and respect for what is going on in their school. All of the teachers at Warren have found this to be a positive strategy for professional development.

Visitation may be informal or part of a more formal peer coaching program. Of primary importance are the goals set by the individual teachers. As principals, we may suggest that a teacher visit another teacher's classroom, but our "suggestion" must not be perceived as a negative evaluation. Requiring a classroom visitation will never ensure that a teacher will take advantage of the experience. With choice comes empowerment. And with empowerment comes responsibility.

There are a variety of ways we use to free teachers to observe and learn from one another. The most beneficial is to hire a substitute for at least one full day to allow a teacher to visit a number of classrooms. Occasionally one substitute covers two or three different classes during the day as the teachers are consecutively freed to observe. At other times, another teacher or the principal relieves classroom teachers.

Consultants

Bringing in experts from outside the local learning community can introduce new ideas into the group and provide impetus for reflection and change. We always make sure that what these consultants present is consistent with our school goals and that they demonstrate a thorough grounding in language-learning research and child development.

Consultants need not come only from the ranks of university professors, publisher representatives, or professional consultants who make their living by traveling from school district to school district selling their programs and materials. We have experienced great success using authors, illustrators, and storytellers who have been recommended by local children's bookstore owners and reading association members. We are also able to "preview" many potential consultants when staff members and we attend national and state conferences of such organizations as the International Reading Association, National Council of Teachers of English, National Association of Bilingual Education, American Library Association, and the Whole Language Umbrella.

Through an informal network of colleagues, we share information about successful classroom teachers, librarians, and principals in the area who are grounded in real school experiences. They make wonderful consultants, and their consultancies are generally more successful, because they can work with our staffs over time rather than give a one-shot workshop.

We are least successful when we impose "professional development" on the teaching staff. Teachers are learners who must have control of their own learning process. Sometimes we are required to bring in district-required consultants who describe district programs and are sent into the schools to provide inservice that is neither requested nor appreciated. Other times we have seen high-powered consultants in action, become really excited about their ideas, invited them to our schools without getting input from the staff, and been disappointed when the consultants are not as well received as we had imagined. Time and again we must go back to our knowledge of how everyone learns—when the experiences are authentic and important to them.

Teacher Study Groups

One of the most effective ways to promote professional development is voluntary teacher study groups (Short et al. 1992). Both of us have successfully supported teachers' learning and change through their participation in study groups. Here are some reasons study groups work so well:

1. Teachers are in control of their own learning. They set the agenda for their study group in collaboration with other educators; it is not a top-down decision.
2. Study groups mesh theory and practice; teachers plan activities based on what they know about learning and curriculum.
3. Study groups provide the time and opportunity in teachers' action-filled schedules for reflection on teaching and learning. As Dewey ([1938] 1972) indicated, reflection allows learners to organize ideas for future use.
4. Teachers see themselves as decision makers who have the power to make changes in their teaching through their own reflection and actions.

5. Teachers' confidence in themselves and their colleagues grows because study groups support both individual professional growth and the development of a strong community of learners.

6. Study groups offer opportunities for growth to teachers at all stages of experience and in all levels of concern. They support those who are struggling and lack confidence in their teaching and push experienced teachers to think through new issues.

7. Principals have the opportunity to provide instructional leadership and support teacher development.

8. Change is seen as a natural part of educators' professional lives, not as an indication that something is "wrong" with teachers and their work.

9. Study groups demonstrate collaborative learning environments in which teachers are able to experience as adults the processes they are trying to create in their own classrooms (Matlin and Short 1996).

Back in August 1990, Dr. Kathy Short of the University of Arizona was discussing with Myna new formats for classroom teaching and learning and teacher change (Matlin and Short 1991). Kathy introduced Myna to an article on study groups by Luis Moll (Moll et al. 1990) and encouraged her to think about establishing one at Warren. The study group started as voluntary and has remained voluntary. Over the years, every teacher has participated for at least a brief time and more than half have remained constant members. Here is one way to get a study group started:

1. Introduce the concept at a faculty meeting. Invite all teachers to attend the study group, and announce where and when it will meet for the first time. Make it very clear that participation is voluntary.

2. Devote the first session to establishing procedures and brainstorming possible topics for the study group to consider. Have the teachers list their concerns and questions on the chalkboard, discuss the issues that might be the most productive for them to pursue, and then decide the initial topic. Also have them establish meeting times and place(s) for the semester. Study groups can meet during lunchtime, after school, or later in the evening over dinner; sometimes classes can be dismissed early.

3. Start each group meeting with sharing, which gives the participants a chance to hear what is going on in other classes. The time for this may vary from very brief to much longer depending on what is happening in classrooms, the school, or the district. Sharing is important because it builds a sense of community, removes teachers' and principals' feelings of isolation, provides the opportunity to celebrate together, and develops support for one another. (At the beginning of a year, each participant can share what he or she is doing differently this year than in the past.)

4. Make sure topics and questions for each successive session are initiated by the teachers. They may be taken from the original list generated at the

beginning of the year or directly from the present needs of the group. A topic may be changed at any time to accommodate a new district mandate or a crisis at school or if teachers are just no longer interested in it.

5. Follow a format that meets the needs of the members. Some groups read and discuss books or journal articles, making connections to their own classes. Some, like those at Warren, focus on reflection and allow all the discussions to develop within the group. When the topic calls for it, teachers bring in materials—including portfolios and field notes, children's literature, adult multicultural literature, professional articles—to share and discuss.

6. Select a facilitator or study group leader to keep the conversation flowing and to summarize comments. (It is important for principals not to facilitate beginning groups, or the study group may be seen as another top-down form of inservice program.)

7. Discuss and set the agenda for the next time at the end of each session. At least fifteen minutes before the end of the session, have the facilitator recap the current discussion and ask for suggestions for the next time.

8. Reconfirm the topic for study at the beginning of the following session before discussions begin.

The Warren study group meets biweekly for one and a half hours after school in the library. Someone always brings snacks. In the beginning we were fortunate to have Kathy Short facilitate the group, because she is an expert at drawing out conversation and teachers' beliefs. She allowed the focus to remain totally on teachers' questions and teachers' learning while demonstrating successful group facilitation strategies. Gradually Kathy became a part of the group and teachers took over facilitation and leadership when they were ready and had found a topic they wished to facilitate. Now that Kathy has left the study group, she remains a mentor and colleague to many of the teachers and to Myna.

Myna has been a member of the study group from the beginning. Originally not all teachers were comfortable with her membership, because they saw her as the "boss" and their evaluator. By working hard to establish herself as a peer and a co-learner, eventually she was accepted as a member of the group. Myna intentionally did not facilitate the study group until well into the fourth year in order to maintain her position as a peer.

One element important to all the study group members (including Myna and Kathy) is confidentiality. Often reflections on and discussions of professional articles or changes in district policies carry over into personal concerns. What is discussed in the group remains there; no information is carried back to central administration, other principals, or other teachers. The trust and mutual respect that have been built in the study group now permeate interactions throughout the building, even those with faculty who are not active members of the study group.

The study group provides a true professional development experience for the teachers and principal at Warren. Topics have included:

- Developing portfolios.
- What is whole language—is it just a fad?
- Literature study groups.
- Assessment and evaluation.
- Organizing classrooms.

Early on, conflicts that had been brewing for years came to the surface. As the study group continues, Myna has seen a greater tolerance for different points of view and actions. Finally, trust and respect have grown. The study group provides each individual the foundation from which to learn and plan together as a staff and take responsibility for his or her own decision making.

Borton staff members recommend professional articles of interest to each other, and meet for informal "brown bag lunches" to share reactions and discuss content. These discussions are valuable, particularly as they tie in to schoolwide goals that are affecting the community—working with AD(H)D children, exceptional education inclusion models, moving toward multiage classrooms, expanding second language opportunities for English-only students.

Principal Study Groups

Our bottom line is that paperwork and similar management duties must be relegated to a lower priority when students, staff, and parents are in the building. We delegate to our wonderful support personnel or take care of issues "after school." This means stress and long hours for us as principals, yet we are committed to building regular formal and informal discussions and meetings with our peers into our schedules.

Voluntary principal study groups are powerful vehicles for supporting the change process and collegial learning. At the same time principals have the opportunity to build community by talking together and "letting it all out" in an environment that is safe and supportive, among others who understand the complexities and demands of the principalship.

Here are some of the reasons study groups work for principals:

1. Sharing and collaborating help solidify views of professional development and establish a renewed respect for the time, energy, and thought that teachers put into everything they do, even those lessons that fall apart as we observe.
2. Principals have a chance to clarify their thinking about teaching and learning—as Myna says, "to know what's in my head." For her it brings out issues about decision making and how inclined she is toward taking an authoritarian stance. Both of us find opportunities to identify and reflect on

conflicts in beliefs within the school district—differences in the philosophy on which curriculum, learning (especially literacy learning), assessment, and testing practices are based.

3. In our hectic jobs, study groups provide an opportunity to talk about teaching and learning. We hear of the solitary nature of the teaching profession, yet principals are even more isolated, often having no one else in the building with whom to talk over certain educational issues. The confidential and privileged nature of study group conversations have given us the community of learners we need.

One of the most successful principal study groups in our school district was one built around Ralph Peterson's *Life in a Crowded Place* (1992). Principals came together one morning a week for ten weeks to discuss our personal reflections about the book and talk with our peers about strategies and ideas that support community building within our district and individual schools.

The format for our group is similar to that of the teacher study group at Warren, and Kathy Short has been an active facilitator and participant.

The success of the principal study group has caused the superintendent to provide additional time at district meetings to share and discuss successful strategies. The study group continues using articles, books, and personal experiences as vehicles to promote reflective learning.

Decision Making

Decision making in whole language schools is shared and collaborative. Three areas in which decision making plays an important role at Borton and Warren are:

- Hiring.
- Faculty meetings.
- Planning.

Hiring

In districts where principals are fortunate enough to do their own hiring, interviews provide the first opportunity to learn about a prospective teacher's prior knowledge and experiences with regard to child development, learning theory, children's literature, the writing and reading processes, thematic instruction, and content area strengths. Interviews also reveal personal qualities like intelligence, flexibility, organization, commitment to school community, ethics, and sense of self as a learner.

We believe it is always important for all constituencies of the school community to take part in the interviewing process. Certainly staff members and parents should be involved. Interview teams may include the principal, teachers, white- and blue-collar support staff, parents, and students. Students also may provide input through the student council, or classes can brainstorm lists of qualities and questions they want to ask prospective teachers, custodians, cafeteria managers, and monitors.

Team interviews give all members the opportunity to be part of the decision about what the job requires and what questions to ask. Questions that may prove helpful in interviewing include:

- What are your views on whole language? Tell us how you would organize your language arts program.
- What would a day in your classroom look like? Be specific.
- We have some classrooms with desks and some with tables. Which would you prefer and why? How would you arrange them and why?
- Thematic teaching and content area instruction includes mathematics, science, fine arts, and social studies. What areas are your strengths? Briefly describe how you would teach in one of your areas of strength.
- Demonstrate a minilesson in literature or writing with a group of students. (Applicants must be asked in advance to be prepared to do this.)
- Request that applicants bring and discuss portfolios of units they have taught; include photographs and examples of students' work.

Faculty Meetings

Faculty meetings at Borton are held every Wednesday after school. The meeting rotates from classroom to classroom and that classroom's teacher runs the meeting. The agenda is put together by the office staff, and members of the staff may request time on the agenda. The general agenda is:

1. Joys and Sorrows—People share specific happenings, vignettes, and concerns; discuss kids needing special attention; and announce special needs.
2. Sharing—The host teacher shares a strategy or successful practice that is working well. Just being in one another's rooms gives everyone the opportunity to ask questions and celebrate individual strengths. It also is an authentic reason to keep classrooms orderly and aesthetically pleasing—because company's coming.
3. Library Update—The librarian has five to ten minutes of every meeting to introduce new books, displaying them and giving a quick book talk. This way, all books are checked out by staff members on the spot. Everyone learns about new resources vital to their professional decision making.
4. Anyone and anything else—General announcements and "administrative stuff" go last. Bob adds what he needs to say, but the gist is written on the agenda. Individual teachers volunteer to take notes for missing colleagues on their agendas and then make a copy.

Faculty and staff meetings are an important venue for solving the day-to-day problems that come up. We also arrange for part-day or whole-day substitutes several times each year so that everyone has an inservice/planning/decision-making time together. These day-long events include all staff members, including custodians, monitors, and food service personnel whenever possible.

Planning

Interacting and planning with community members, parents, staff, and students is one of the most important aspects of any principal's job and cannot take place in isolation. It involves a sensitivity to people—their personalities, cultures, feelings, and views about specific issues (discipline, for example) and the world in general. All constituents are stakeholders in education; we therefore attempt to involve them in planning, decision making, and the educational process.

We make every effort to encourage authentic input at staff meetings, parent meetings, and committee meetings. Even the best staff and most cooperative parents need training in and experience with consensus building and conflict resolution in these formalized structures. Otherwise, it is too easy for those who disagree to argue and prevent productive discussions or to stay quiet and raise issues and torpedo innovations long after we believe agreement has been reached. Even after training, it is helpful periodically to revisit the concepts of consensus building and conflict resolution.

Staff members from both schools have successfully implemented their own versions of brainstorming techniques in which individuals assign priorities to a brainstormed list and come to a group consensus. The process requires several large sheets of butcher paper, markers, tape, and a facilitator and/or a recorder. It is very helpful if the school goals are prominently posted, so that the group can remain focused on the school vision. The process takes some time to implement in the beginning, but with experience, the staff and parents (and students) become very efficient. Here's how we do it:

1. We discuss the issue. Each person in turn has a chance to share concerns, make suggestions, or identify the crux of the problem. These responses are recorded on flipchart paper, not a chalkboard that will be erased. It is often necessary to revisit the original problem statement and early comments.
2. Everyone takes several minutes to reflect in silence and then write down possible solutions and approaches. Quiet reflection is critical to helping people focus their thoughts, but it is the most difficult part of the process to facilitate, because people have a hard time dealing with silence when they are eager to solve a problem.
3. After several minutes, the parameters for brainstorming are clearly stated and agreed on so that there will be no negative comments or put-downs. Then each person in turn has a chance to share possible solutions. Every

idea at this stage is given equal weight. The recorder writes those responses on a second piece of butcher paper for all to see.

4. After all the responses are listed, the group combines similar responses or asks people to clarify their solutions. Again the process proceeds through each person in turn. This is an important step, because it makes each participant responsible for understanding the possible solutions.

5. The revised list of responses is rewritten on another sheet of paper and displayed. The facilitator then reviews the original concerns and asks for final discussion.

6. Next each participant writes down their first, second, and third choices.

7. Each participant in turn identifies their first, second, and third choices as the facilitator records the corresponding weighted scores (third choice, 1; second choice, 2; first choice 3). The weighted scores are then totaled.

8. The totals may reflect a clear consensus, or several solutions may be equally popular. If there is not a clear consensus, the group undertakes final negotiations to resolve the issue.

9. The facilitator asks each participant in turn whether he or she can live with the group consensus. (Sometimes we ask for volunteers to meet separately to iron out details.)

Topics we have taken through the process include:

- How the remainder of a budget line will be spent.
- What the focus of a staff study group will be.
- The lunch schedule and configuration.
- Curriculum goals for the year.
- PTA activities.
- Theme study choices.
- The professional development calendar for the year.

This process is especially effective when the community is in an uproar over a concern that is broad and not easily defined or when the "daily gossip" includes solutions that are incompatible with school goals.

Dear Dr. Matlin,

The reason why I haven't been back at Warren was because I moved to New Mexico with my family. I moved to a tiny town called Socorro. It was nice. There was a canyon and stream called Water Canyon. We went to Water Canyon every week. I played with my dog in the stream. I'm glad to be back at Warren now. I missed everyone including you Dr. Matlin.

Sincerely,
Andrea

SEVEN

Interacting with Families

Principals have always invited and encouraged families to come to school for open houses, parent conferences, fund raisers, to help with clerical and housekeeping chores, or to solve problems when their kids "mess up." These are all fine—and necessary—activities. As whole language principals we have the additional challenge to engage families (and staff members) at all levels of decision making. If we as principals are truly committed to educational reform, we must involve families and community members throughout the process. We must reflect and expand on our traditional notions of what is meant by "parental involvement."

Often, administrative rhetoric encourages families and staff members to have a "voice" in the school when what the principal really wants is for them to stay out of her hair and agree with her methods. We find that our greatest challenge is learning to listen to the differing viewpoints in our communities and to respond with a variety of learning strategies that will involve these alternative voices in productive dialogue.

The best teachers promote a feeling of pride in their students, a feeling that prompts these students to do their personal best. They encourage their students to take responsibility for their own learning and support the learning of others. This process is based on building trust and maintaining continual communication among students, teachers, and families. Principals are no less responsible for establishing similar relationships at the school level. One of our primary roles as whole language principals is to foster feelings of ownership and empowerment in our students' families.

We cannot afford to be seen as distant, haughty, or condescending administrators who are dictating programs and curriculums without giving all stakeholders, family members included, opportunities to be part of the process. Yes, not every parent sees things from a whole language perspective. And yes, sometimes we have to compromise our short-range goals for change. And yes, we still need to find ways to promote further dialogue on those issues that we see as hurdles to the process.

We cannot become incapacitated by fear of conflict and disagreement. We cannot control the thinking and actions of others, but we do control how we interact with others. In our school district, one very wise administrator, Becky Montaño, explains to community members, "The schools that we, as adults, attended did a great job of preparing us to be good citizens and live in the world today. Now schools must look different and teachers must teach differently to prepare our children for the world they will face in the future."

Our credibility with families depends on the strength of our convictions, our ability to articulate our beliefs, and the trustworthy manner in which we conduct ourselves. We work with other adults in the school community to find ways to agree to disagree and move forward in finding common ground in our shared goals for supporting students' learning.

We make it a point to hear families' concerns immediately. The longer a parent "stews" over a concern, the bigger the confrontation will ultimately be. Often, a quick on-the-spot conversation can keep an issue from growing out of proportion. Hearing and quickly acting on issues raised at home and in the community is a large part of our responsibilities. This involves returning telephone calls quickly, attending all parent functions, and being around just before and after school, when parent traffic is high.

Family math nights, family literacy nights, and family science nights have been huge successes. Groups of teachers collaborate to give families and children the chance to participate in activities that help them understand a curricular area and the pedagogical techniques and strategies being employed. Our participation at these events demonstrates our knowledge of curriculum areas and makes us accessible to parents who have specific concerns.

Parent Teacher Association (PTA) or other parent organization meetings are also opportunities to meet parents and strengthen communication. We sometimes read aloud at these meetings—books that present a specific perspective or invoke a personal response to a point we would like to make. Some of our favorites are listed at the end of this chapter.

What Works?

Empowerment and true parent participation require frequent formal and informal opportunities and contexts in which principals, teachers, and families can talk together. Many families are uncomfortable coming to school because their own school experiences have been negative. Here are a few strategies that facilitate parental involvement and support:

- Greet *all* families with a smile and an authentic welcome. Even when it is not easy, there is *always* something nice you can say, especially when you know your students and can say something positive about them.
- Thank family members for being at school and ask them to return often.
- Try out a few words of greeting and common phrases in languages other than English that are spoken by families in the school. They will appreciate your efforts. If you are like us and stumble a bit, parents will see that you are human and make mistakes when you are learning, just like they do.
- Take advantage of every occasion to share something positive and specific about their child. Just as you encourage teachers to make contact with families early in the school year, you should also establish rapport before any concerns are raised.
- Return parents' and concerned community members' telephone calls *the same day* whenever possible.
- Have a specific place where coffee is available and make sure parents, other visitors, and volunteers know about it. Many schools have designated parent rooms where volunteers find helpful hints to promote learning on bulletin boards, a cup of coffee, and a list of specific jobs that will help out the school. Be creative and ask local markets and restaurants to donate the coffee; make sure there is a sign saying "Courtesy of So-and-So."
- Promote monthly "Coffee with the Principal" sessions. One principal we work with serves coffee and sends everyone home with a coffee mug with the school name and telephone number on it. At Warren a refrigerator magnet containing the telephone number of the school is given to school visitors and people who join the parent organization.
- Initiate informal chats in the hallway or on the playground when families arrive before and after school.
- Include family members on all hiring committees, interview teams, planning committees, and facilities committees.
- Rotate when you schedule meetings and special events: before school, during school, after school, on weekends. This way all families will be able to participate in some functions.

■ Provide a variety of functions for families to attend: curriculum discussions, parenting classes, substance-abuse-prevention workshops, T-shirt-painting workshops, craft classes, cooking activities. The not-specifically-school-related activities are often better attended and give you a chance to initiate conversations about raising your own kids. Soon you are sharing parenting strategies in a nonthreatening manner. This informal sharing strategy may become an entree into more significant and meaningful dialogue on issues we normally discuss with the same parent participants over and over again.

■ Help every staff member (teachers, teaching assistants, office staff, custodians, food service workers, monitors, and crossing guards) see themselves as ambassadors for the school and as vital to setting a tone of welcome for families.

■ Encourage office personnel to be warm and empathetic on the telephone: they represent the school. Demonstrate how to listen to angry parents, and allow them to vent their anger before asking for details. (There are also one-day professional seminars designed to help office personnel deal with angry constituents.)

■ Encourage teachers to have a special corner in each classroom where families can read posted bulletins and notes that did not make it home.

First and Lasting Impressions

We encourage all our teachers to make every effort to contact each student's family during the first ten days of school to share something positive and specific about that child. (This is especially necessary if we suspect we will need to contact families about concerns later in the school year.)

This can be as simple as a teacher's telephoning to say, "I just had to call and tell you what a special help Elizabeth was in class today. She not only cleaned up quickly after math, but helped several others finish and clean up as well. I am so proud of how well she cooperated and took responsibility for the classroom. I'm happy she's in my room this year." This establishes that the teacher cares about the student and sets a tone of high expectations.

First impressions are equally important for principals. We try to have a smile and a hello for everyone we meet. It's important for principals to let families know we care. Since we can't possibly call every family in the school, we focus our energies on kindergarten families and the families of other students new to the school. Myna greets new families at fall registration and tries to be in the outer office when new families register during the year. This is definitely easier when families register first thing in the morning, but it is well worth the effort wherever it falls in a day because positive rapport is established immediately. Bob's contact may be a telephone call, a note through the school postal system, or a personal greeting as the students are dropped off or picked up.

We both review the school goals and our views on learning and teaching with new kindergarten families in May, when they have their orientation for the fall. Bob shares Cambourne's conditions for learning (Chapter 2) and shows examples of writing from four-, five-, and six-year-olds to help families see learning as a continuum rather than a start-stop operation. Myna describes the similarities between learning to write and read in school and early oral language learning at home: parents can easily relate to examples of children's learning to say Mama or Papa. We both take the opportunity to plant the seeds of our schools' philosophy regarding bilingual education and multiage classes. This sets a tone and expectation for the entire time their children will attend the school.

In the fall most principals host open houses. Bob has a special kindergarten open house to share his whole language philosophy, present the Borton school goals, and show how daily activities at Borton are consistent with his beliefs about how children become lifelong learners. In addition to a fall open house, during January the teachers at Warren invite parents and students to come to school to visit classrooms, examine students' work portfolios, and discuss work in progress. Myna visits each classroom at some point during the evening and is in the front hall encouraging conversation as everyone is leaving.

Written Communication

It is helpful if all written communications—office notes, weekly homework assignments, and classroom newsletters—go home on the same day of the week. At Borton all families know that notes go home on Mondays, so they expect some sort of school communication (see Figure 7.1) every Monday. The "Monday note" routine has worked so well at Borton over the years that Myna and the Warren teachers have adopted the procedure too. (That's a nice way of saying that they stole the idea, but isn't that what all principals do?) The responsibility to take notes home is the child's. No one can complain that they didn't get information: when notes don't come home on Monday, it's the family's job to ask their child where the notes are.

Myna and a parent from the school applied for and received a minigrant from a local educational foundation to publish a monthly newsletter. There is a column written by the principal, monthly announcements, news features, stories by students, and letters to the parent editor. Bob sends out weekly newsletters in English and Spanish each Monday. Both languages are given equal weight, presented on either side of a single piece of paper. These types of school bulletins share upcoming events and acknowledge the efforts of staff members, students, and families to make our schools better places in which to spend our precious time. It is one way of maintaining constant communication with families, and we "fill in" with little tidbits of parenting advice and our shared goals and expectations for the school.

We encourage all teachers to send home regular monthly or weekly newsletters that celebrate what is being learned and informs families about what is going on in their children's classes (see Figures 7.2 and 7.3). That way when Susan is

BORTON BULLETIN   May 10, 1993

Thanks to all of our parents and staff for a wonderful Cinco de Mayo fiesta! Our small school grossed $1,800.00. That will pay for our symphony program next year and an additional author visit.

Staff inservice: We are having one last staff inservice this Wednesday, May 12th, for staff and interested parents. It is the follow-up workshop for consensus training that will provide structure for our future Site Based Decision Making committee meetings. Parents are invited. There will be substitutes in classrooms.

Artist-in-Residence: A special thank-you to writer Will Clipman, our Artist-in-Residence for the past four weeks. We are fortunate that the PTA sponsors this experience for our children and staff. We were poets—and now we know it!

Third-Grade Picnic: The third graders and their teachers (and the principal!) will be going to Golf-N-Stuff on Monday, May 17th. We will leave Borton at 9:30 A.M. and return at approximately 2:00 P.M. We will be using private transportation. A special THANK-YOU to the Student Council for sponsoring this special event. Please contact your child's teacher if you can help drive.

End-of-the-Year Assembly: We will have an end-of-the-year assembly on Tuesday, May 18th, at 1:00 P.M. in the cafeteria. Parents are welcome to attend this special ending to a very special year. The staff will put on our annual play for the kids. This year it will be "Too Much Noise." And of course there will be music and special good-byes to our graduating third graders.

Class Placement Reminder: Your child's classroom placement for 1993–1994 will be on the report card that will go home on the last day of school. We cannot guarantee a parent's first choice. Please share any specific educational concerns in writing with the placement committee. The office will be open until Tuesday, May 25th, and will reopen Monday, August 2nd. Mail will be delivered throughout the summer to 700 E. 22nd St., Tucson, AZ 85713. All concerns will be reviewed the week prior to the beginning of school and you will be contacted if a change is possible. Thanks for your patience in helping us keep our classrooms ethnically and gender balanced.

No Extended Day on our last day of school Wednesday, May 19th. All children will need to be picked up, walk home, or leave on the early bus. Have a safe and restful summer. Keep in touch.

Bob Wortman

Dates to Remember

THIRD GRADE TRIP TO GOLF-N-STUFF—Monday, May 17th—sack lunches
END-OF-THE-YEAR ASSEMBLY—Tuesday, May 18th, 1:00 P.M. in cafeteria
STUDENTS' LAST DAY—Wednesday, May 19th—NO EXTENDED DAY

FIRST DAY OF SCHOOL IS MONDAY, AUGUST 16th

Figure 7.1   Borton parent newsletter.

THE BALLOON ROOM

The Balloon Room

Borton Primary Magnet School

September 7, 1993

The Balloon Room

Teri Melendez   Graciela Ortiz

OPEN HOUSE

We will be having an open house on September 14th from 6:30-7:30p.m. Dr. Wortman will make some announcements in the patio and then he will dismiss to classes. This is the time for your child to show you around the room. It is also a good time to ask any programmatic questions you may have. Please remember that it is not a good time to inquire as to the progress of your child. Hope to see you here next Tuesday.

CENTERS

The children are continuing to work on the centers listed last week. They will not be done today because of the holiday. We do not have centers on Wednesday, so they will be done on Thursday. We will not start new centers on Friday since it is easier for the children to remember if they have two days to get started before the weekend.

PTA REPRESENTATIVES

We have gotten a couple of maybes but no YES, I'LL DO IT!s from all of you. To be a representative is basically to attend monthly meetings and sometimes to call parents to help with PTA functions. Usually it does not require a lot of time and is easier if 2-4 people volunteer. Please think about it and let us know right away if you can help out.

STUDENT COUNCIL REPRESENTATIVES

The children voted last week for student council representatives. The two elected were Paige Salzbrenner and Vincent Olea. They attended their first meeting last week and will periodically be meeting with Dr. Wortman to discuss school issues.

SNACK AND COOKING FUND

Please remember to send in $5.00 for September if you have not already done so. Thanks.

DONATION RECEIPTS

Your receipt is attached to this letter for any money received since August. We will always staple the receipts to the newsletter in order to try to assure that they are getting home. Many people use these receipts as evidence of donations to a non-profit organization for their taxes. If you have sent in money and do not receive a receipt by the next week, please let us know.

THIS YEAR'S THEMES

The children have narrowed down the choices and will make their final decisions this week with a big vote and tally on Friday.

HOMEWORK POLICY AND TOOLS

It is important that homework not be stressful. If you find it to be, please let it go. Homework is voluntary and can be adjusted to fit each individual child's needs... for example: child 1 has parents do all recording of information, child 2 draws pictures and parents fill in words, child 3 does developmental writing (beginning sounds, letter strings, pretend writing...) and parents help record (for the teacher) and child 4 uses developmental writing that approximates standard spelling enough to read. All are acceptable. Please do not force your child beyond the point where s/he is functioning at any given time. Just as children walk and talk at different times so do they acquire academic skills and more refined developmental skills at different rates.

If you do not have supplies at home for your child to do homework, please let us know. Generally what is needed is glue or paste, scissors, crayons and paper. We can send home paper and used crayons. A type of glue can be made with small amounts of flour and water.

HOMEWORK

Look around your home for all the different shapes that you see. Draw them and cut them out and paste them on the large colored paper. Bring it to school when it is finished.

Figure 7.2   Sample Borton class newsletter.

Newsletter 9

August 16, 1994

Welcome!

Room 9 would like to welcome back returning students and offer a special hello to students who are new to our school. A few students are also new to Tucson,(they are really receiving a "warm" welcome). This is the first of many newsletters which will update you on all our activities. We are in the process of getting to know students and arranging their schedules to meet their individual needs. As soon as I can get all the information and specialist schedules, I will be sending parents their child's schedule. If there are any special concerns or equipment needed, please contact me at school 578-4640. Along with their schedule, I will send a list of any needed supplies. Unless I have already contacted you, your child only

needs a backpack. Keep in touch, Cristina Franco-Carrillo

Meet the Staff

Dolores Arenas and Yvonne Templeton are the paraprofessionals in room 9. Dolores has been at Warren 6 years, Yvonne for 3 years. Both bring with them a wealth of experience and knowledge of special education. We are lucky to have them working with us and sharing all their expertise.

Wanted: Ideas to share in our newsletter

If you have a suggestion, activity, book title, recipe, cartoon, etc. that you would like to share, please send it in to Room 9. We'd be happy to print it.

Figure 7.3   Sample Warren class newsletter.

asked, "What did you do in school today, dear?" and she answers "Nothin'," the parent may say, "Well, I see in your class news that you are studying rain forests . . ." That is usually enough to prompt more specific information from children to let their families know that, indeed, there is a lot of learning going on.

Newsletters help develop a learning community comprising both home and school, and if this basic level of communication is in place, the principal's job of supporting the teaching staff in their risk taking is easier. It is especially helpful when parents are concerned about innovative ideas and techniques that are different from what they perceive as traditional school activities.

Newsletters don't have to be fancy, but they do need to be informative and to the point. They always need to convey the message that children are the school's reason for existing and that school personnel are accessible, sensitive, and willing to work in partnership with families.

Books to Read with Parents and Community Members

- *Your Own Best Secret Place,* by Byrd Baylor (1986). Exemplifies the power of community in the school. Encourages families to view school as a special place to maintain and share with others.
- *Frederick,* by Leo Lioni (1967). Highlights the importance of identifying and using everyone's gifts to the community.
- *On the Day You Were Born,* by Debra Frazier (1991). Shows the power of feeling welcomed and accepted into a community.
- *The Signmaker's Assistant,* by Tedd Arnold (1992). Reminds us it is important to think critically before automatically believing everything in print.
- *Tales of the Perfect Child,* by Florence Parry Heide (1985). Details classic cases of child behavior and the way they control adults. Helps adults laugh at common "problems" with children.
- *Will I Have a Friend?,* by Miriam Cohen (1989). Reminds us of the importance of supporting friendships and belonging to a group.
- *First Grade Takes a Test,* by Miriam Cohen (1980). Reminds us that there are forms of evaluation other than traditional tests.
- *When Will I Read?,* by Miriam Cohen (1987). Reminds us that there are alternative paths to literacy development that are individual and specific to each child.
- *Leo the Late Bloomer,* by Robert Krause (1971). Exemplifies the developmental nature of learning and that each child is an individual.
- *My Great Aunt Arizona,* by Gloria Houston (1992). Provides a powerful example of the nature of teaching and the power that loving and supportive teachers have in the lives of children.

Dear Mr. Wortman You are
a Gratl Gratl Prensable
and I liKe Your TeOase
liKe Pica up the trash and
Do not fiut You are
TR e fe t
from Gabe

CHAPTER
EIGHT

Evaluation and Whole Language

Within the word e*valu*ation is the word *value*. Society assesses that which it values in individuals, teachers, students, and schools. And principals evaluate that which they know and value. From our standpoint as whole language principals, evaluation isn't a summative assessment of where we are—rather, it is an ongoing formative process reflecting how far we have come and where we need to go next.

Student Evaluation

Since Ralph Tyler (1949) wrote about curriculum and evaluation, educators have realized its significance in the teaching and learning processes. As "lessons are taught," both teaching and learning strategies are assessed to see how well students learn concepts and how a teacher's interactions with students need to be modified to help students learn more effectively.

We strongly believe that this ongoing, formative assessment of both teaching and learning improves the quality of education for students. We encourage using work samples, portfolios, conferences, teacher observation and field notes, checklists, and criterion-reference tests, among other means, to provide important evaluation data on each student's learning. Questions that guide student eVALUation are:

1. What can the child do?
2. How does this inform your instruction of the child?
3. Why are you evaluating this aspect of the child's learning (What is the value)?
4. What is the purpose and who is the audience for the evaluation?
   a. Student self-evaluation.
   b. Evaluation of child for instruction.
   c. Assessment of learning to plan the next steps to be taken.
   d. Reporting to parents.
   e. Reporting to the community.
   f. Teacher self-evaluation and goal setting.

Multiple Data Sources

In *Creating Curriculum* (Short and Burke 1991) Carolyn Burke writes about the variety of audiences and purposes classroom assessment serves—from lawmakers and the general public to parents, teachers, and students. She makes a strong argument for aligning the type of assessment with its intended use, audience, and purpose. One of the best means of student evaluation is observation by a knowledgeable classroom teacher. Taking time to step back and observe students gives teachers the opportunity to see students in the process of learning as well as to observe interactions, evaluate the context established for learning, and determine the next steps that will support future learning. Look to the following data sources for student evaluation criteria:

- Logs of books read.
- Favorite poems, songs, and chants.
- Writing samples.
- Anecdotal records.
- Informal/formal observations.
- Audio/video samples.
- Notes from individual reading/writing conferences.
- Checklists of literacy development.
- Miscue analysis or running records.
- Interest inventories.
- Student surveys/interviews/checklists/comments.
- Parent surveys/interviews/checklists/comments.
- Literature responses that reflect student's growth as a reader.
- Written work that reflects student's growth as a writer.
- Journal entries.
- Copies of reports.
- Webs/charts/lists that reflect what has been learned.

Teacher Observations and Assessment

Within every classroom, we expect to see a variety of formative and summative evaluation strategies occurring on an ongoing basis. Evaluation is carried out in a variety of contexts in order to establish the most appropriate learning environment for all students and to obtain a more complete picture of children's abilities and strengths. Language learning is assessed during mathematics and fine arts as well as during literature discussions and writers workshop.

As children work in large groups, teachers assess which children stay on task, which are confident enough to risk speaking out or to lead a group, and which use group support to learn. Teachers use large-group interactions to evaluate their teaching strategies by observing how students respond, how interested and involved students remain, and what needs to be followed up in small groups or individually.

More intensive evaluation, called kidwatching by Yetta Goodman (1978), takes place when teachers observe students in small groups or pairs. These observations yield information for evaluating development and planning future instruction.

Evaluating lessons and learning structures within the classroom also provides information to teachers about how to use space effectively. Observing students working on their own helps teachers see how each learner develops and uses strategies for writing, reading, and thinking. Chapter 6 describes the many ways we support teachers in learning new assessment techniques and building time into their instructional day to kidwatch.

Learning and Test Taking

Over time, the definition of evaluation has narrowed to mean *standardized tests* to the community, and as principals and educators, we have a responsibility to help our students succeed in all ways that will make them successful in school and in the larger society. While neither of us philosophically believes in using only one measure of summative evaluation to assess learning, we do comply with our district testing guidelines and encourage all teachers to give standardized testing serious attention and to practice "testwise" strategies with students.

Assessment Myths and Misconceptions

To understand the assessment and evaluation strategies needed to analyze students' learning and classroom interactions, we need to look at some of the common myths and misconceptions held by the public (and often the educational community) as identified in *Evaluating Literacy* (Anthony et al. 1992):

1. *Assessment and evaluation are separate from instruction.* We believe the most powerful evaluation informs instruction and serves as a scaffold to future learning. Traditionally the educational community has used decontextualized measures designed by outsiders to assess what children know or don't know and to report student progress to those outside the classroom. If evaluation is to have any use at all, it must assess what children can do so that teachers may make educational decisions that allow children to continue growing.

2. *Language is learned hierarchically; therefore, it should be tested sequentially.* The past forty years of research in language learning has demonstrated that oral and written language development are sociopsycholinguistic processes that are idiosyncratic and different for each child. Although there are similarities in how children learn to read and write, no one hierarchical structure for the development of concepts meets the needs of all children. Publishers and testing companies establish unique activity and assessment sequences not based on their knowledge of how children learn but in order to be different from other publishing companies.

3. *Tests tell us what children know.* The context for traditional standardized test taking has been that of summative evaluation in the form of true-false, multiple-choice, fill-in-the-blank, and circle-the-correct-answer formats. These measures make it easier to score large numbers of students quickly, and, more important, produce data that are mathematically manipulable. But to believe that a multiple-choice test is a comprehensive assessment of students' knowledge and abilities is naive at best. Tests may provide teachers with some useful data, but overall they provide only a small part of a comprehensive evaluation of students as learners.

4. *Evaluation is testing.* We see evaluation as the compilation of many kinds of data that provide educators with a view of students as learners. Tests reveal specific responses to specific questions; these responses do not provide a broad view of students and learning. Evaluation requires the additional information provided by contextualized observations of performance, interviews, self-evaluations, and other data sources.

5. *Standardized tests are objective measures of performance.* Standardized tests are based on the assumption that intelligence and human behavior can be quantified and evenly distributed across a normal curve in the same way physical characteristics of size and weight were described by scientists at the turn of the century. We reject the notion that children distribute "normally" across a first through ninth Stanine ranking, and our discussion here cannot begin to encompass the existing literature on cultural and linguistic bias in tests. We believe that all children learn and deserve to be viewed in the context of their full potential—not automatically designated above or below a hypothetical midline that has been manipulated by statisticians to describe children as "smart" or "dumb." Standardized measures have been developed by "experts" who focus their energies on maintaining an even distribution of responses on

individual test items, subtests, and overall measures. Educators all know that as test scores rise over time, individual test items are revised to *trick* some children into choosing incorrect items so that the normal curve is perpetuated.

6. *Teacher observations are neither valid nor reliable.* The publishing and educational establishment have systematically and effectively convinced generations of parents and teachers that teachers' professional knowledge and capabilities for assessing student growth are inadequate. In the best scenario, teacher assessment is viewed as subjective and less valuable than the "objective" measures of standardized assessments. In the worst situations, teacher assessment is completely discounted. As a result, we now have some teachers who believe they are incapable of evaluating children effectively without using decontextualized instruments. They "view" the child through a test, rather than use the information gained from a test as one aspect of their professional ability to observe and gain new insights into the learner. We believe that a knowledgeable teacher's observations and professional decision making are powerful tools for instructional planning and for assessing student progress.

7. *Outsiders know better than teachers and parents about the progress of children.* We believe that teachers, as members of the classroom community, are in the best position to assess students. Teachers use their knowledge of learning, curriculum, individual children, and the classroom as a social setting to evaluate learning and teaching. Whole language teachers see such evaluation as a continuous part of their teaching responsibilities.

Resources

We encourage teachers to share new evaluation techniques as an integral part of their professional development. At Borton, one teacher learned to do miscue analysis, a holistic assessment of student reading process, several years ago. Slowly but surely teachers are learning to do their own modified miscue analysis with students. Bob takes classrooms in order for a teacher to observe how the procedure is done. (For more information about miscue analysis, see *Reading Miscue Inventory: Alternative Procedures,* by Goodman, Watson, and Burke 1987.)

Many books and district guides are available to each principal who wishes to read more about student evaluation. We list resources we have found valuable in Chapter 9 and will not reproduce all the wise words of other authors here. Nevertheless, we want to stress the absolute importance we see in student evaluation and assessment.

Teacher Evaluation

Everyone is a learner—children and adults alike—and evaluation is an integral part of teachers' learning processes, just as it is with students. Every aspect of teaching and learning is analyzed or evaluated to provide scaffolding for future learning—to continue to move ahead as learners. Teaching happens first in the minds of teachers, and as teaching changes, teachers and principals must be deliberate and reflective in their evaluation of classroom practice and their organization of the school. Evaluation, indeed all learning, is a collaborative process that supports authentic change and growth. As school administrators, our role is to support teachers in this developmental learning process.

At the same time, the procedures for and purposes of evaluating teachers in our school district, as in most, are mandated by state law and the negotiated teachers' agreement. The evaluation procedure and documents are clearly defined, and the school administrator is ultimately responsible for complying with the laws and guidelines. Unfortunately, such a formalized, standardized procedure sometimes leads principals to focus their energies on their role as *evaluators* to the exclusion of their role as *curriculum leaders* and *lead teachers* in their schools.

In our district, teachers are rated on a check sheet in:

1. Planning and preparation.
2. Implementation of curriculum and instruction.
3. Student assessment and evaluation.
4. Classroom effectiveness.
5. School/systemwide effectiveness.

The ratings are "meets/exceeds," "partially meets," and "does not meet." There is little opportunity for written comments and responses.

Because we believe in the unique abilities and knowledge of each teacher in our schools, we have adapted the existing summative-based teacher evaluation into one that is more comprehensive and formative. We have incorporated the ideas, forms, and support of other administrators who have shared better ways to evaluate teaching and learning. We value the opportunity to have had such interactions.

Teacher evaluation by a whole language principal may follow the outward appearance of clinical supervision models while at the same time always reflecting the ideals of:

■ Supportive environments for mutual respect, risk taking, and growth.
■ Acceptance of and support for individual differences.
■ Belief in learning through collaboration.
■ Patterns of growth built on an individual teacher's strengths.
■ Strong commitment to staff development.

Setting Expectations

In a whole language school, students are viewed as individuals having unique areas of competence who need a safe, supportive, and collaborative environment in which to learn. These same concepts are true for the adult learners in the building. The way teachers were evaluated in the past stemmed from the notion that they were "finished products" when they graduated from college, not lifelong learners. They were either "good" or "bad" teachers and often nothing was done to support professional development (and change). The current more holistic views of teaching and learning view teachers' growth in the same way as students' learning.

All teachers are individuals; all teach differently. All have strengths and areas in which they need to continue to grow. Expectations for each teacher reflect his or her professional and personal best. Whole language teachers, like whole language principals, have explicit goals that take into account their

- Teaching philosophy and belief system.
- Knowledge of learning theory and child development.
- View of their classroom as a social entity.
- Individual students' needs.
- Professional growth.

Goals for teacher growth are developed in a collaborative manner at both schools (see Chapter 6). Each spring at Warren, the entire staff works together to develop school goals for the following year, goals that are action-oriented and based on student, staff, and community needs. At that same time, Myna meets with teachers individually to establish their personal goals for growth during the next school year. These goals are negotiated to reflect both the needs of the teacher and the needs of the school. Spring goal setting is beneficial, because it provides direction to the school, puts the vision out in front for everyone to see.

Preobservation Conferences

In our district, the evaluation process is presented to the faculty before the school year begins, as mandated in the teachers' contract. We also hold individual preobservation conferences that are quite informal and set the tone for the scheduled observations. Teachers tell us their goals and their plans for what we will see during the observation session. Many teachers prefer that we observe them "teaching the whole class," which sometimes translates into lecturing to the class. Yet there is much to be learned when we observe teachers working with students in a variety of settings—large groups, small groups, pairs, or one-to-one. We encourage many different types of interactions during our observations.

Observing Teachers at Work

Observing teachers in the classroom once or twice a semester is an artificial device to meet the requirements of state or district mandates. When we visit classes frequently, teachers and students are comfortable with the visits and continue their normal interactions. Our visits are "not a big deal." Because of our many visits, we have a good idea of what is going on in each classroom. The formal observation simply becomes a showcase for the teachers' strengths. Teachers set their own times for formal observations to show us their "very best." Some teachers invite us in to see a new strategy or concept they are trying and on which they would like our reactions and comments.

During the formal observation, we script much of the teacher-student interaction. At times we script student-student interactions. As principals, we have the luxury of observing the class as a whole system. Teachers often do not have the time to step back to gain this perspective. By sharing our whole-class perspective with them, we help teachers reflect on their class as a community of learners.

Assessing Classrooms

When we walk into classrooms, we want them to demonstrate the following qualities:

- *Ownership by the children.* We expect the work of children to dominate. All children should have their work displayed—not just the "best" but the real everyday work. Bulletin boards and displays should be created by kids for their own purposes. Bob tells teachers that he would prefer that the bulletin boards be empty when school starts and filled with the work of children by the end of the first week rather than have commercial materials as the primary visual images in the classroom.
- *Richness of content.* We expect to get a good sense of the themes children are studying. The books, materials, and displayed works by students should reflect the science, mathematics, social sciences, humanities, and fine arts themes of the curriculum.
- *Pleasing aesthetics.* Although we tell parents that we don't want our classrooms to be formal living rooms, we also explain to teachers that when company comes we straighten up. Visitors provide authentic reasons for the staff to maintain organized and appealing classrooms. We expect children's work to be displayed beautifully and with pride. Plants, striking displays of children's artwork, and art prints, make powerful visual statements and help children develop a sense of audience in new contexts.
- *A healthy social and emotional climate.* We expect kids to feel respected and free to take the risks of sharing their written and oral ideas. They should not fear public embarrassment or ridicule. We expect teachers to be good role models, to demonstrate how people of all ages treat one another. Norms for the classroom are posted so that the teacher can help students focus on the social necessity for maintaining a supportive and positive environment. There are discussions about the parameters for living and working together collaboratively. Interactions among students and teacher reflect the agreed-on goals of the classroom.

- *Literacy.* We expect a variety of books and displays, representing a range of genres, to be available to children at all times. Songs, poems, recipes, lists, illustrations, diagrams, encyclopedias, dictionaries, maps, content area texts, and literature books provide resources for learning, and we expect to see them in constant use.

The Evaluation Process

As whole language principals, we evaluate staff within the context of how successfully we meet our own goals. As we demonstrate our beliefs and goals in daily interactions with the people we supervise, we set the tone for successful and positive evaluation. The actual process follows the district-required procedures, but with a few additions of our own.

Observations. We try to do *walk-throughs* every day. Bob might stick his head into classroom doors and wink or nod at kids without interrupting the classes, or Myna might walk around the classroom talking with individuals or groups about their work and offering encouragement. Bob writes anecdotal records of classroom interactions; Myna uses a checklist to which she adds her comments (see Chapter 3). We talk to teachers every day about what's happening in their classrooms.

Teachers sometimes ask us to evaluate a specific lesson, but in general they prefer to be evaluated within the context of the informal observations we have described. When we are in and out so often, our "official" evaluation observations become just one more piece of data and no one is particularly nervous about it—teachers and kids just do what they always do when we are in the room.

Conferences. Teachers must have access to the principal. If we are not in our office, teachers leave us notes. We always attempt to follow up the same day. Many one-legged conferences, as Gene Hall (Hall and Hord 1987) calls them— brief discussions and suggestions given on the run—happen throughout the day.

We usually conduct two formal, individual conferences with teachers each year. Bob's first formal "talk-over" occurs the fourth or fifth week of school. Myna's takes place after the first formal observation in October or early November. She tries to schedule conferences one to two days after formal observations. This gives the teachers and her time to reflect on the teaching/learning process yet the experience is still fresh.

Formal conferences are about an hour long. We discuss the professional goals written by the teacher the previous May and identify resources needed to meet those goals. We then discuss the principal's role in helping teachers work toward meeting their goals. We also go through the class list and discuss the progress of individual students. This helps teachers focus on their students as individuals, helps us know the students through the eyes of their teachers, and identifies any "red flags" to be followed up with the Child Study Team.

The second evaluation is formally documented as the summative evaluation for district purposes. Together we review anecdotal records, classroom newsletters, and checklists collected over the year and any parent notes that include specific data for discussing strengths. We discuss the degree to which the year's goals have been accomplished and negotiate the goals for the following year. This part of the process makes the evaluation formative and personal to the teachers, rather than strictly summative and judgmental. We automatically assume that every teacher has the professional responsibility to reflect on strengths and areas for growth. Every teacher, no matter how wonderful, is always learning new techniques and new knowledge. The goals that we set together are not written in stone; they may expand or narrow as either the teacher or we recommend.

The Evaluation Form.   We use our formal school board–approved evaluation instrument and add to it. Bob and his teachers write in "(Teacher's) Goals for the School Year" and then list three specific goals. He requires at least one curricular goal. Examples of Borton teacher goals include:

- Institute writers workshop a minimum of forty-five minutes, three times per week.
- Expand use of math manipulatives.
- Begin work on master's program.
- Observe literature studies in other classrooms.
- Have every child publish four books during the year.
- Institute author's chair as part of writing time.
- Involve students in group planning meetings.

Myna uses a portion of the existing form, "Areas Recommended for Growth" to focus on areas agreed on between her and the teacher. She requires no set number of goals, and negotiates the choices with each teacher. Warren's teachers' goals are quite similar to those of Borton teachers. One goal usually relates to a schoolwide focus such as implementing questioning and wait-time strategies to increase students' thoughtful reflection. There is never enough room on the form to write recommendations, and we add pages as necessary.

When teachers need to improve, we both use a specific section of the form entitled "Areas Recommended for Improvement" to document the teacher's needs and our support for his or her improvement. Again, we always feel free to expand on the district form.

Myna uses the "Evaluator Comments" and "Evaluator Recommendations" sections to highlight teachers' strengths. Bob changes these headings to "Principal's Goals," and then collaboratively he and the teacher he is evaluating choose several goals for Bob that will support the teacher's professional growth. Examples include:

- Model four writers workshop minilessons in September.

- Take over class so teacher can observe other teachers' science activities.
- Organize large-group experiences for students so teachers can take part in collaborative planning sessions with other teachers.
- Arrange for a substitute so teachers can visit other multiage classrooms.
- Help create a text set for sanctuary theme immersion.
- Contact science department to arrange for loan of science equipment.

We encourage the teachers to write something in the space provided for "Teacher Comments." Traditionally this space is used to rebut a negative evaluation. We think teachers should use it to make a few self-evaluative statements about their own learning; as such, it becomes a powerful validation for personal professional growth.

We are still in the process of refining our roles in teacher evaluation, and we often ask for "reality checks" at faculty meetings to make sure our actions reflect our intent. We see positive results—in the curriculum and in the faces of children—when teachers are allowed to build on their strengths and to select and monitor the changes in their own practice. We become not just an overseer of a school, but a fully participating member of the learning community.

Supporting Teachers' Learning

The most important support we provide teachers is demonstrating that we believe that they are working to the best of their abilities as knowledgeable professionals. We establish an environment that recognizes the dynamic nature of change as integral to the learning process. We support teachers in decision making and provide resources and encouragement when they attempt change. This view of principal and teacher collaboration in evaluation has brought about powerful changes in both professional development and planning at our schools.

Older models of professional development usually had experts coming into a school or district to "change" the teachers. After we began to participate in the evaluation process, it became clear that sharing, negotiating, and collaborating are powerful elements for supporting teacher assessment and that these same elements build the learning and professional development of educators.

From their discussions about evaluation in the teacher study group, Myna and the Warren teachers realized they needed to change the way they planned their teaching. Because at least half the staff found writing traditional weekly lesson plans frustrating, they started a new process of quarterly goal setting and self-evaluation. Now most teachers look at planning in larger, more holistic ways. They write their curricular goals and expectations for nine-week periods and share them with Myna. Daily schedules and plan books more accurately reflect what is going on in classrooms; lessons are written for the teachers, not for the principal.

Assessing Whole Language Principles in the School

(Answer yes, no, partially, or not sure.)

WE ARE A COMMUNITY OF LEARNERS.
_____ Principal and staff establish a safe climate for learning.
_____ Students, teachers/staff, and principal are viewed as learners.
_____ It is okay to make mistakes.
_____ District curriculum is implemented.
_____ Team planning and grade-level planning occur regularly.
_____ Professional decisions are made by teachers.
_____ Staff development is planned by teachers, staff, and principal.
_____ Invitations are extended to parents to participate in shared decision making.
_____ Intergenerational programs bring community members into the school.

EVERYONE SUCCEEDS/LEARNS AT OUR SCHOOL.
_____ The potential of all students is VALUED.
_____ There are many experiences and opportunities for success.
_____ Alternative grouping strategies are employed.
_____ Rules for learning are developed collaboratively in each classroom.
_____ Students and staff are encouraged to help each other learn.
_____ All students' work is displayed publicly.
_____ Students and staff take responsibility for maintaining an attractive learning environment.
_____ Special Education students are integrated into classrooms.
_____ Learning is not fragmented—whole teachers teach whole students.
_____ Teachers know what students know and start there to enhance their knowledge.
_____ The principal starts where learners are to enhance their knowledge.
_____ The principal accepts the use of existing practices and helps expand the teachers' repertoire.

IN OUR LITERATE ENVIRONMENT EVERYONE LEARNS TO COMMUNICATE.
_____ Reading occurs across the curriculum.
_____ Writing occurs across the curriculum.
_____ Teachers focus on the process of reading.
_____ Teachers focus on the process of writing.
_____ Students have access to a wide range of literacy materials.
_____ Fiction and nonfiction literature are important components of the reading program.
_____ Reading strategies are learned in context.
_____ There are many opportunities for conversations about curriculum in the classrooms.
_____ There are many opportunities for informal conversations in the school.
_____ Strong library support is available.
_____ Books are available all around the school.

ALTERNATIVE ASSESSMENT IS USED TO SUPPORT THE LEARNING PROCESS.
_____ Assessment provides information about the learning process.
_____ Informal and formal assessments are used in classrooms.
_____ Teacher- and student-constructed tests are used to measure students' learning of specific content.
_____ Samples of student work provide documentation of learning.
_____ Written learning samples, as well as audio and video samples, are used.
_____ Observation and anecdotal records provide information about teaching and learning.
_____ Standardized tests are acknowledged as public measures of achievement.

Myna L. Matlin/1992

Figure 8.1 Assessing whole language principles in the school.

Principal Evaluation

True evaluation of students informs instruction and true evaluation of teachers informs practice. As whole language principals we recognize that self-reflection is the most powerful form of principal evaluation. We deliberately make sure that our vision and goal statements are congruent with our beliefs about teaching and learning.

We are required to participate in an extensive administrative evaluation system that incorporates vision statements, school goals, standardized test results, and the information on satisfaction surveys completed by parents and staff members. We both prepare portfolios to share with the assistant superintendent at our formal evaluation conferences. These portfolios contain:

- An updated vita that lists professional affiliations, activities, and awards.
- Client satisfaction survey results.
- The district administrative evaluation instrument.
- Our professional goals for the year with written self-reflection.
- Schoolwide goals.
- A listing of staff professional development activities for the year.
- A listing of parent, community, and district committee activities for the year.
- Correspondence from parents, staff, students, and visitors that reflect their assessment of their experiences.
- Copies of media coverage for the year.
- Photos of us interacting with students, parents, staff, and community members.

Bob also includes:

- Samples of minutes from the Site Based Decision Making CORE Committee.
- A list of professional books and articles that he has read.

Before meeting with the assistant superintendent, Myna does an assessment of the whole language teaching and learning at Warren. She uses a checklist that she developed earlier in her principalship to find strengths and areas for needed growth (see Figure 8.1). She focuses her support and future goals on these areas.

Evaluation is central to whole language schools and integral to the learning process. Each day our decisions and interactions grow out of our assessment and evaluation of the school climate, classrooms, discipline, professional development, and parent participation. Our evaluative eye directed through a whole language lens improves teaching and learning at our schools.

Principals' roles as instructional leaders require that they continually update their knowledge and remain reflective, well read, open-minded, articulate, and eager to share ideas and views. Just as evaluation is important to the learning of students and teachers, we accept it as essential to our personal and professional growth as whole language principals.

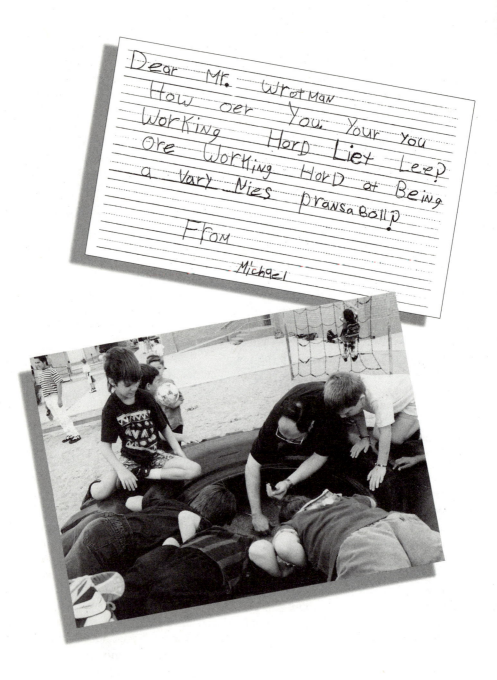

Dear Mr. Wrotman
How oer You. Your you
Working Hord Liet Leep
ore Working HorD at Being
a Vary Nies pransaBolld.

From

Michael

NINE

Questions We Are Asked
About Whole Language

As classrooms and schools introduce more holistic practices, parents, community members, staff members, and other principals ask hard questions that need to be answered thoughtfully and respectfully. We end our book by responding to some of the questions about whole language that we are most frequently asked. (The appendix lists the resources we have found most useful.)

How Do You Encourage a Teacher to Move to Whole Language?

The most difficult challenge principals face is how to encourage and support real change. The research of Gene Hall (Hall and Hord 1987) and Michael Fullan (Fullan and Pomfret 1977) shows that forced change never lasts. Teachers can always give a new idea or program lip service and then close their doors and do as they have always done. Their plan books may even document what looks like a whole language curriculum—but it is what they do with students that counts. As principals we continually remind ourselves that published programs do not teach. If we want to change instruction, we support change in the *heads and hearts of teachers*. Unless teachers view themselves as learners, they will continue to use programs, put children through their paces, and blame the kids when they do not learn the material.

Whole language principals believe that adults learn the same way children do—by building on prior knowledge and strengths in an environment where risk taking is encouraged and supported. Every teacher in the building has a different belief system and unique experiences. Whole language principals accept teachers where they are, focus on their strengths, and encourage them to take instructional risks in areas of both strength and needed growth. Teachers make gains by building on their strengths, whether those strengths are in science, math, or fine arts.

Whole language principals establish climates that support teachers as they take risks. It's always important for teachers to know that their principal respects them as professionals and understands that they really are good at their jobs. When they feel safe from the ridicule and judgmental remarks of community members and peers, teachers will try out new practices and instructional techniques.

To discuss teacher change, Bob uses the metaphor of the swimming pool. Some teachers are very comfortable diving in headfirst and treading water in the deep end immediately. Some can jump in, but need to get out right away and dive in somewhere else. Some teachers slip into the deep end and hold onto the side as they adjust to the change. Others wade in from the shallow end a few steps at a time. They take long pauses when they reach waist or tummy level and have the hardest time getting their head underwater. There are always those who watch, ask about the water temperature, and need to be enticed and supported before they will get wet at all.

The most difficult are those who never get into the pool but always tell you what expert swimmers and divers they are. Some outside force always keeps them from joining their colleagues for the swim, but they are always there poolside, taunting them about their backstroke and splashing water in their faces. Sometimes, too, the most proficient are the most impatient with the progress of their colleagues.

To support these differences there must be continual opportunities for teacher observation and dialogue. And the dialogue and reflections are most useful when they are site specific. Teachers need to see other teachers demonstrating the techniques they want to adopt. They need time to reflect and talk with their peers about questions and concerns. They may do this through formal university course work, professional conferences, or district workshops.

School-based staff development strategies are usually the most successful and encourage the most teacher buy-in and ownership. Strategies that we have found most useful are more fully developed in Chapter 6 and include teacher study groups, mentoring, and informal support groups.

Are Whole Language Classrooms the Same as Open Education Classrooms?

Whole language is not open education. There are some similarities because both movements developed from similar roots. Both are grounded in the writings of educational reformers such as John Dewey ([1938] 1972). Open education certainly supported schools in looking more closely at the impact of affective environments and the power of small-group learning, project approaches to collaborative learning, and multiage groupings.

Unfortunately, the professionals implementing open education were seldom grounded in language-learning research. They did not fully embrace constructivist learning principles. The individualized approach of programmed instruction combined with the center approach more often than not reduced learning to a specified hierarchy of subskills learned in isolation. Team teaching was often reduced to "turn" teaching, and the curriculum was still segmented along traditional behaviorist lines.

Isn't Whole Language Just a Fad?

Holistic practices have always been used. Educators will always debate whole-to-part learning versus part-to-whole learning: the behaviorist and constructivist paradigms are different.

The power of whole language is that it has emerged as a grass-roots movement by teachers and principals who accept responsibility for their teaching. They make instructional decisions that are consistent with their beliefs about learning and the knowledge of their individual students. They recognize the benefits of good literature and a content-rich curriculum. They will not easily return to simplistic textbooks and disconnected worksheets.

Experts in specialized educational fields are embracing the basic tenets of whole language as well. Professionals in special education, second language learning, gifted education, diversity education, and compensatory education are realizing the power of using real texts in authentic settings. The name may change, but teachers will never again willingly rely on boring and limiting materials. Rich literature, writing across the curriculum, and integrated instruction will not go away.

The challenge is to help teachers continually reflect on their practice and be deliberate in their instructional decisions. Every publisher and fly-by-night consultant in the country is advertising their materials and approaches as whole language. But whole language can never be reduced to a commercial program or published set of materials. As explained more fully in Chapter 2, whole language is a philosophy and belief system based on current research about literacy and learning.

Isn't Whole Language Something That Only Good Teachers Can Do?

Good teachers have been using all manner of approaches and materials for years. Whole language helps good teachers become outstanding teachers because it invites their creativity and supports their professional autonomy. Change takes time and each teacher grows professionally on different paths—some in children's literature, some in writers workshop, and some in science. Whole language principals recognize the unique journeys that teachers and staff members need to make and provide structures and support to encourage change.

Another way to answer this question is, All teachers are supposed to be good teachers. If they aren't good teachers, there is another path for the principal to take. Documenting and counseling teachers who are not capable of meeting the rigors of effective teaching are not pleasant tasks. But principals are responsible for the evaluation and stewardship of the school community. Being whole language principals doesn't mean that we are nice to everyone and allow kids and teachers to run amok. It means that we are dedicated to the profession and are willing to make hard decisions about the health of the community. Adopting a whole language philosophy will not make the problem teachers go away.

What Do You Do About Other Teachers Who Aren't Doing Whole Language?

Whole language isn't something you fall into. It is an individual process of growth. Some teachers with a well-articulated traditional philosophy and classroom style have been successful for many years. But students and the system are changing. It becomes even more imperative that principals establish norms for the school that invite communication while accepting individual differences among staff members.

If teachers are "worth their salt," they probably have some curricular strengths and some practices in place that a principal can use as points of departure for discussing self-reflection, goal setting, and teachers as learners.

Although many teachers get a master's degree as quickly as they can, few pursue post–master's degree programs. They often do not have the time or energy to enroll in graduate classes in teaching and learning. Their professional growth is often accomplished via disconnected conference sessions, workshops, and professional discussions with their peers. Principals need to recognize the gap that exists between teachers working on degrees and those pursuing professional growth by alternative means. This is why most principals are always on the lookout for ways to encourage teacher learning through study groups and other site-specific means.

The Kids Are Learning, but How Do You Prove They're Learning?

The entire educational community is wrestling with assessment and evaluation. Whole language principals recognize that society eVALUates that which is valued. Principals need to talk with teachers and parents about the many ways of documenting learning other than formal tests.

Testing can be like taking a child's temperature when she's not looking well. The thermometer registers normal, but the school nurse can tell there's a problem. Society traditionally has assumed that when kids and schools have high test scores the teaching and learning are satisfactory, that test scores and learning are directly correlated. But we know this is not the case. Most outstanding teaching and learning occur in areas traditional tests are not able to measure.

We deal more fully with assessment in Chapter 8; however, data sources that we use to document successes include:

- Observations, anecdotal records, and teacher field notes.
- Client satisfaction surveys completed by parents and students.
- Children's writing.
- Samples of children's work over time.
- Lists of children's reading and writing activities.
- Library circulation records.
- Attendance records.
- Classroom discipline referrals.
- Reading miscue inventories or running records.
- Standardized tests.
- Performance-based assessments.

What About Skills?

What is a skill? How does a skill relate to performance and competence? When a carpenter constructs a table, it is difficult to break down the finished work into its individual components because each component makes sense only within the context of the whole experience. To reach a high level of proficiency, carpenters do not plane pieces of wood day after day, then spend hours practicing their sawing. They become experts through much the same process Cambourne (1988) suggests for learning to speak, read, and write at home and at school.

Skills are learned best in context. They are learned in the process of authentic work—where there is purpose and where the activity would happen in real life.

We have helped others understand this point by using variations of this exercise:

1. Ask parents or teachers who are concerned with learning skills to list *all* the skills that are important for being a proficient reader.
2. Ask them to prioritize and discuss these skills as they relate to being a life-long reader and writer.
3. Ask them to identify aspects of the environment and interactions with others that support emerging readers.

The lists usually include few of the generalized "skills" in traditional workbooks, basal programs, or teacher exercises. Traditional phonics and grammar rules are always farther down the list of priorities, with items such as "comprehension" at the top. And seeing parents reading books at bedtime are examples of experiences that always emerge.

How Do Special Education Programs Function in a Whole Language School?

Traditionally, special-needs students and their instruction were isolated from the learning mainstream. Those students least prepared to adjust to frequent changes in their learning environment were pulled in and out of the classroom or simply removed altogether. Students having the most difficulty with isolated skill programs received more of the same, year after year.

Today the law demands that special education students be included in regular classrooms and that their learning be integrated into the classroom program. Educators are recognizing that special education teachers and school psychologists must be knowledgeable about oral and written language learning. Special-needs students must be viewed through different means than traditional standardized measurements. Whole language classrooms are organized to expect a range of learner abilities, diverse languages and cultures, and differing interests and beliefs.

Don't Bilingual Children Learn Differently?

It is difficult for whole language principals not to become embroiled in the politics of bilingual education; this is now a prominent issue in the United States and around the world. We believe that the status of a language is imposed by society, not by inherent superior characteristics. In our schools, where English and Spanish are the dominant languages, we work hard to provide second language learning for all students. Both languages are given equal weight in newsletters and in the school office.

Over the past twenty years, second language research by Barbara Flores (1982), Carol Edelsky (1986), and many others has demonstrated that all written languages, like spoken languages, are learned in similar ways. These researchers have helped educators understand the misconceptions about some languages being more phonetic than others and needing more emphasis on phonics. Children learn to read and write in all alphabetic languages (e.g., Spanish, German, English) in similar ways.

Whole language bilingual classrooms are organized heterogeneously so that students are not "tracked" by ability or language use. Language is used in natural contexts throughout the day. Students learn a second language through meaning. Concepts are introduced in a child's home language with the understanding that first language semantic, syntactic, and graphophonic strengths will carry over and support reading and writing in the second language. A curriculum rich in content helps students develop literacy strategies more easily: it is easier for them to read and write about what they have experienced and know. This is true for anyone learning a new language.

Whole language bilingual teachers use cultural sensitivity, kidwatching strategies, and their knowledge of teaching and learning to make educational decisions. They are masterful at organizing curriculum and instruction to provide a variety of purposes and audiences so that language is used in natural contexts. Efficient second language learning requires that students have the opportunity to interact with proficient language users and a variety of authentic materials in the second language.

There are numerous books on bilingual education in whole language classrooms. We list some in the appendix and encourage interested principals to read further.

What About the Parents? Will They Understand?

Parents want their children to be successful in school. They may not visit often because of their work schedule, a lack of transportation, their own uncomfortable experiences with schools, or other reasons. But the majority of parents want to know that their children are happy in the classroom, that the teachers know their kids and treat them fairly, and that the teachers are *good* teachers.

Principals are responsible for helping parents understand the process of school change. Parents must develop ownership in the school, just as the staff does, and realize that schools will never again look the way they did in the fifties, sixties, or seventies. The kids won't let that happen.

Teachers and principals must be able to show student progress through student work. Educators must convey everything that is being done in the school to support children in their learning. Changes must be discussed in terms that communicate without being condescending. When learning is discussed like this, parents see for themselves the similarities between learning to talk and learning to read and write.

Where Can You Find More Information About Whole Language?

There are a great many books and journals that discuss whole language principles from a variety of perspectives and fields of study. The appendix lists some of our favorites.

Dear Dr. Matlin,
I couldn't write to you
because we have to write
in journal only I like to
write to you and you like
to write to me it is fun.

Your friend,
Jimmy

Appendix

Books on Whole Language Principles

Whole Language Teaching and Learning

Cambourne, B. 1988. *The Whole Story: Natural Learning and the Acquisition of Literacy in the Classroom*. New York: Scholastic.

Edelsky, C., B. Altwerger, and B. Flores. 1991. *Whole Language: What's the Difference?* Portsmouth, NH: Heinemann.

Goodman, K. 1986. *What's Whole in Whole Language?* Portsmouth, NH: Heinemann.

Goodman, Y., D. Watson, and C. Burke. 1980. *Reading Strategies: Focus on Comprehension*. Katonah, NY: Richard C. Owen.

Harste, J., K. Short, and C. Burke. 1995. *Creating Classrooms for Authors and Inquirers*. Portsmouth, NH: Heinemann.

Short, K., and C. Burke. 1991. *Creating Curriculum: Students and Teachers as a Community of Learners*. Portsmouth, NH: Heinemann.

Whole Language and Beginning Readers

Avery, C. 1993. *And with a Light Touch: Learning about Reading, Writing, and Teaching with First Graders*. Portsmouth, NH: Heinemann.

Fisher, B. 1991. *Joyful Learning: A Whole Language Kindergarten*. Portsmouth, NH: Heinemann.

Holdaway, D. 1979. *The Foundations of Literacy*. New York: Scholastic.

Ministry of Education, Wellington, New Zealand. 1985. *Reading in Junior Classes*. Katonah, NY: Richard C. Owen.

Mooney, M. 1990. *Reading to, with and by Children*. Katonah, NY: Richard C. Owen.

Whole Language and Older Students

Atwell, N. 1987. *In the Middle: Writing, Reading, and Learning with Adolescents*. Portsmouth, NH: Heinemann–Boynton Cook.

Benedict, S., ed. 1992. *Beyond Words: Picture Books for Older Readers and Writers*. Portsmouth, NH: Heinemann.

Cordiero, P. 1992. *Whole Language and Content in Upper Elementary Grades*. Katonah, NY: Richard C. Owen.

Rief, L. 1991. *Seeking Diversity: Language Arts with Adolescents*. Portsmouth, NH: Heinemann.

Whole Language and Second Language Learners

Edelsky, C. 1986. *Writing in a Bilingual Program: Habia una Vez*. Norwood, NJ: Ablex.

Freeman, Y., and D. Freeman. 1992. *Whole Language for Second Language Learners*. Portsmouth, NH: Heinemann.

——. 1994. *Between Worlds: Access to Second Language Acquistion*. Portsmouth, NH: Heinemann.

Rigg, P., and V. Allen, eds. 1989. *When They Don't All Speak English*. Urbana, IL: National Council of Teachers of English.

Whitmore, K., and C. Crowell. 1994. *Inventing a Classroom: Life in a Bilingual, Whole Language Learning Community*. York, ME: Stenhouse.

Whole Language and Special-Needs Students

Phinney, M. 1988. *Reading with the Troubled Reader*. Portsmouth, NH: Heinemann.

Rhodes, L., and C. Dudley-Marling. 1988. *Readers and Writers with a Difference: A Holistic Approach to Teaching Learning Disabled and Remedial Students*. Portsmouth, NH: Heinemann.

Stires, S. 1991. *With Promise: Redefining Reading and Writing Needs for "Special" Students*. Portsmouth, NH: Heinemann.

Taylor, D. 1990. *Learning Denied*. Portsmouth, NH: Heinemann.

Weaver, C., ed. 1994. *Success at Last! Helping Students with Attention Deficit (Hyperactivity) Disorders Achieve Their Potential*. Portsmouth, NH: Heinemann.

Organizing Whole Language Classrooms

Crafton, L. 1991. *Whole Language: Getting Started . . . Moving Forward*. Katonah, NY: Richard C. Owen.

Goodman, K., L. Bird, and Y. Goodman. 1991. *The Whole Language Catalogue*. Santa Rosa, CA: American School.

Goodman, Y., W. Hood, and K. Goodman. 1991. *Organizing for Whole Language*. Portsmouth, NH: Heinemann.

Mills, H., J. Clyde, and V. Woodward. 1990. *Portraits of Whole Language Classrooms: Learning for All Ages*. Portsmouth, NH: Heinemann.

Peterson, R. 1992. *Life in a Crowded Place: Making a Learning Community*. Portsmouth, NH: Heinemann.

Routman, R. 1991. *Invitations: Changing as Teachers and Learners K–12*. Portsmouth, NH: Heinemann.

Literature in the Classroom

Cullinan, B., ed. 1987. *Children's Literature in the Reading Program*. Newark, DE: International Reading Association.

Harwayne, S. 1992. *Lasting Impressions: Weaving Literature into the Writing Workshop*. Portsmouth, NH: Heinemann.

Johnson, T., and D. Louis. 1988. *Literacy Through Literature*. Portsmouth, NH: Heinemann.

Peterson, R., and M. Eeds. 1990. *Grand Conversations: Literature Groups in Action*. New York: Scholastic.

Pierce, K., and C. Gilles. 1993. *Cycles of Meaning: Exploring the Potential of Talk in Learning Communities*. Portsmouth, NH: Heinemann.

Short, K., and K. Pierce. 1990. *Talking About Books: Creating Literate Communities*. Portsmouth, NH: Heinemann.

Writing in the Classroom

Calkins, L. 1983. *Lessons from a Child*. Portsmouth, NH: Heinemann.

———. 1990. *Living Between the Lines*. Portsmouth, NH: Heinemann.

———. 1994. *The Art of Teaching Writing*. 2d ed. Portsmouth, NH: Heinemann.

Fletcher, R. 1992. *What a Writer Needs*. Portsmouth, NH: Heinemann.

Graves, D. 1983. *Writing: Teachers and Children at Work*. Portsmouth, NH: Heinemann.

Thematic Instruction

Baker, D., C. Semple, and T. Stead. 1990. *How Big Is the Moon? Whole Maths in Action*. Portsmouth, NH: Heinemann.

Doris, Ellen. 1991. *Doing What Scientists Do: Children Learn to Investigate Their World*. Portsmouth, NH: Heinemann.

Grandberg, R., W. Kwak, M. Hutchings, and J. Altheim. 1988. *Learning and Loving It: Theme Studies in the Classroom*. Portsmouth, NH: Heinemann.

Manning, M., G. Manning, and R. Long. 1994. *Theme Immersion: Inquiry-Based Curriculum in Elementary and Middle Schools*. Portsmouth, NH: Heinemann.

Steffey, S., and W. Hood, eds. 1994. *If This Is Social Studies, Why Isn't It Boring?* York, ME: Stenhouse.

Wells, G. 1992. *Constructing Knowledge Together: Classrooms as Centers of Inquiry and Literacy*. Portsmouth, NH: Heinemann.

Whitin, D., H. Mills, and T. O'Keefe. 1990. *Living and Learning Mathematics: Stories and Strategies for Supporting Mathematical Literacy*. Portsmouth, NH: Heinemann.

Assessment and Evaluation

Anthony, R., T. Johnson, N. Mickelson, and A. Preece. 1992. *Evaluating Literacy: A Perspective for Change*. Portsmouth, NH: Heinemann.

Goodman, K., Y. Goodman, and W. Hood. 1988. *The Whole Language Evaluation Book*. Portsmouth, NH: Heinemann.

Goodman, K., L. Bird, and Y. Goodman. 1992. *The Whole Language Catalogue Supplement on Authentic Assessment*. Santa Rosa, CA: American School.

Harp, B., ed. 1991. *Assessment and Evaluation in Whole Language Programs*. Norwood, MA: Christopher-Gordon.

Rhodes, L., and N. Shanklin. 1992. *Windows into Literacy: Assessing Learners K–8*. Portsmouth, NH: Heinemann.

Smith, F. 1988. *Insult to Intelligence: The Bureaucratic Invasion of Our Classrooms*. Portsmouth, NH: Heinemann.

Spelling

Bolton, F. and D. Snowball. 1993. *Teaching Spelling: A Practical Resource.* Portsmouth, NH: Heinemann.

Gentry, J. R. 1987. *Spel . . . Is a Four-Letter Word.* Portsmouth, NH: Heinemann.

Wilde, S. 1991. *You Kan Red This! Spelling and Punctuation for Whole Language Classrooms.* Portsmouth, NH: Heinemann.

References

Anthony, R., T. Johnson, N. Mickelson, and A. Preece. 1992. *Evaluating Literacy: A Perspective for Change*. Portsmouth, NH: Heinemann.

Atwell, N. 1987. *In the Middle: Writing, Reading, and Learning with Adolescents*. Portsmouth, NH: Heinemann–Boynton/Cook.

Avery, C. 1993. *And with a Light Touch: Learning about Reading, Writing, and Teaching with First Graders*. Portsmouth, NH: Heinemann.

Baker, D., C. Semple, and T. Stead. 1990. *How Big Is the Moon? Whole Maths in Action*. Portsmouth, NH: Heinemann.

Benedict, S., ed. 1992. *Beyond Words: Picture Books for Older Readers and Writers*. Portsmouth, NH: Heinemann.

Britton, J., A. Burgess, N. Martin, A. McLeod, and H. Rosen. 1975. *The Development of Writing Abilities*. Urbana, IL: National Council of Teachers of English.

Calkins, L. 1983. *Lessons from a Child*. Portsmouth, NH: Heinemann.

_____. 1990. *Living Between the Lines*. Portsmouth, NH: Heinemann.

_____. 1994. *The Art of Teaching Writing*. 2d ed. Portsmouth, NH: Heinemann.

Cambourne, B. 1988. *The Whole Story: Natural Learning and the Acquisition of Literacy in the Classroom*. New York: Scholastic.

Cazden, C. 1988. *Classroom Discourse: The Language of Teaching and Learning*. Portsmouth, NH: Heinemann.

Clark, M. 1975. "Language and Reading: Research Trends." In *Problems of Language and Learning*, ed. A. Davies. London: Heinemann Educational Books.

Cordiero, P. 1992. *Whole Language and Content in Upper Elementary Grades*. Katonah, NY: Richard C. Owen.

Crafton, L. 1991. *Whole Language: Getting Started . . . Moving Forward*. Katonah, NY: Richard C. Owen.

Cullinan, B., ed. 1987. *Children's Literature in the Reading Program*. Newark, DE: International Reading Association.

Curwin, R., and A. Mendler. 1988. *Discipline with Dignity*. Washington, DC: Association for Supervision and Curriculum Development.

Dewey, J. [1938] 1972. *Experience and Education*. New York: Collier.

Doris, E. 1991. *Doing What Scientists Do: Children Learn to Investigate Their World*. Portsmouth, NH: Heinemann.

Dreikers, R., and V. Soltz. 1964. *Children: The Challenge*. New York: Hawthorne.

Durkin, D. 1966. *Children Who Read Early*. New York: Teachers College Press.

Edelsky, C. 1986. *Writing in a Bilingual Program: Habia una Vez*. Norwood, NJ: Ablex.

Edelsky, C., B. Altwerger, and B. Flores. 1991. *Whole Language: What's the Difference?* Portsmouth, NH: Heinemann.

Edelsky, C., and K. Smith. 1984. "Is That Writing—or Are Those Marks Just a Figment of Your Curriculum?" *Language Arts* 61 (1): pp. 24–39.

Fisher, B. 1991. *Joyful Learning: A Whole Language Kindergarten*. Portsmouth, NH: Heinemann.

Fletcher, R. 1992. *What a Writer Needs*. Portsmouth, NH: Heinemann.

Flores, B. 1982. *Language Interference or Influence: Toward a Theory for Hispanic Bilingualism*. Ph.D. diss., University of Arizona.

Freeman, Y., and D. Freeman. 1992. *Whole Language for Second Language Learners*. Portsmouth, NH: Heinemann.

———. 1994. *Between Worlds: Access to Second Language Acquisition*. Portsmouth, NH: Heinemann.

Fullan, M., and A. Pomfret. 1977. "Research on Curriculum and Instructional Implementation." *Review of Educational Change* 47: 335–97.

Gardner, H. 1985. *Frames of Mind: Theory of Multiple Intelligences*. New York: Basic.

Gentry, J. R. 1987. *Spel . . . Is a Four-Letter Word*. Portsmouth, NH: Heinemann.

Gollasch, F., ed. 1982. *The Selected Writings of Kenneth S. Goodman: Process, Theory, Research*, vol. 1. Boston: Routledge & Kegan Paul.

Goodlad, J. 1984. *A Place Called School*. New York: McGraw-Hill.

Goodman, K. 1970. "Reading: A Psycholinguistic Guessing Game." In *Theoretical Models and Processes in Reading*, ed. H. Singer and R. Rudell. Newark, DE: International Reading Association.

———. 1986. *What's Whole in Whole Language?* Portsmouth, NH: Heinemann.

Goodman, K., L. Bird, and Y. Goodman. 1991. *The Whole Language Catalogue*. Santa Rosa, CA: American School.

———. 1992. *The Whole Language Catalogue Supplement on Authentic Assessment*. Santa Rosa, CA: American School.

Goodman, K., and Y. Goodman. 1979. "Learning to Read Is Natural." In *Theory and Practice of Early Reading,* vol. 1, ed. L. Resnick and P. Weaver. Hillsdale, NJ: Lawrence Erlbaum.

Goodman, K., Y. Goodman, and W. Hood. 1988. *The Whole Language Evaluation Book*. Portsmouth, NH: Heinemann.

Goodman, Y. 1978. "Kidwatching: An Alternative to Testing." *National Elementary Principal* 57(4): 41–55.

Goodman, Y., W. Hood, and K. Goodman. 1991. *Organizing for Whole Language*. Portsmouth, NH: Heinemann.

Goodman, Y., D. Watson, and C. Burke. 1980. *Reading Strategies: Focus on Comprehension*. Katonah, NY: Richard C. Owen.

———.1987. *Reading Miscue Inventory: Alternative Procedures*. Katonah, NY: Richard C. Owen.

Grandberg, R., W. Kwak, M. Hutchings, and J. Altheim. 1988. *Learning and Loving It: Theme Studies in the Classroom*. Portsmouth, NH: Heinemann.

Graves, D. 1975. "An Examination of the Writing Processes of Seven-Year-Old Children." *Research in the Teaching of English* 9 (3): pp. 227–241.

———. 1983. *Writing: Teachers and Children at Work*. Portsmouth, NH: Heinemann.

Hall, G., and S. Hord. 1987. *Change in Schools: Facilitating the Process*. New York: State University of New York.

Halliday, M. A. K. 1977. *Explorations in the Functions of Language*. New York: Elsevier North-Holland.

———. 1980. "Three Aspects of Children's Language Development: Learning Language, Learning Through Language, Learning About Language." Proceedings from IMPACT Conferences, ed. Y. Goodman, M. Haussler, and D. Strickland. Washington, DC:

National Institute of Education/International Reading Association/National Council of Teachers of English.

Harp, B., ed. 1991. *Assessment and Evaluation in Whole Language Programs*. Norwood, MA: Christopher-Gordon.

Harste, J., C. Burke, and V. Woodward. 1984. *Language Stories and Literacy Lessons*. Portsmouth, NH: Heinemann.

Harste, J., K. Short, and C. Burke. 1995. *Creating Classrooms for Authors and Inquirers*. Portsmouth, NH: Heinemann.

Hart, L. 1983. *Human Brain and Human Learning*. New York: Longman.

Harwayne, S. 1992. *Lasting Impressions: Weaving Literature into the Writing Workshop*. Portsmouth, NH: Heinemann.

Haussler, M. 1982. *Transitions Into Literacy: A Psycholinguistic Analysis of Beginning Reading in Kindergarten and First-Grade Children*. Ph.D. diss., University of Arizona.

Holdaway, D. 1979. *The Foundations of Literacy*. New York: Scholastic.

Johnson, T., and D. Louis. 1988. *Literacy Through Literature*. Portsmouth, NH: Heinemann.

Kasten, W., and B. Clark. 1993. *The Multi-Age Classroom a Family of Learners*. Katonah, NY: Richard C. Owen.

Kovalik, S., with K. Olsen. 1994. *Integrated Thematic Instruction: The Model*. Kent, WA: Susan Kovalik.

Lester, N., and C. Onore. 1990. *Learning Change*. Portsmouth, NH: Heinemann.

Lindfors, J. 1987. *Children's Language and Learning*. Englewood Cliffs, NJ: Prentice-Hall.

Loughlin, C., and M. Martin. 1984. *Supporting Literacy*. New York: Teachers College Press.

Manning, M., G. Manning, and R. Long. 1994. *Theme Immersion: Inquiry-Based Curriculum in Elementary and Middle Schools*. Portsmouth, NH: Heinemann.

Matlin, M., and K. Short. 1991. "How Our Teacher Study Group Sparks Change." *Educational Leadership* 49(3):68.

———. 1996. "Study Groups: Inviting Teachers to Learn Together." In *Practicing What We Teach: Whole Language Voices in Teacher Education*, ed. K. Whitmore and Y. Goodman. York, ME: Stenhouse.

Mills, H., J. Clyde, and V. Woodward. 1990. *Portraits of Whole Language Classrooms: Learning for All Ages*. Portsmouth, NH: Heinemann.

Ministry of Education, Wellington, New Zealand. 1985. *Reading in Junior Classes*. Katonah, NY: Richard C. Owen.

Moll, L., C. Veliz-Ibanez, J. Greenberg et al. 1990. "Community Knowledge and Classroom Practice: Combining Resources for Literacy Instruction." Unpublished manuscript, University of Arizona.

Mooney, M. 1990. *Reading to, with and by Children*. Katonah, NY: Richard C. Owen.

Peterson, R. 1992. *Life in a Crowded Place: Making a Learning Community*. Portsmouth, NH: Heinemann.

Peterson, R., and M. Eeds. 1990. *Grand Conversations: Literature Groups in Action*. New York: Scholastic.

Phinney, M. 1988. *Reading with the Troubled Reader*. Portsmouth, NH: Heinemann.

Piaget, J. 1965. *The Language and Thought of the Child*. New York: World.

———. 1969. *The Psychology of the Child*. New York: Basic.

Pierce, K., and C. Gilles. 1993. *Cycles of Meaning: Exploring the Potential of Talk in Learning Communities*. Portsmouth, NH: Heinemann.

Rhodes, L., and C. Dudley-Marling. 1988. *Readers and Writers with a Difference: A Holistic Approach to Teaching Learning Disabled and Remedial Students*. Portsmouth, NH: Heinemann.

Rhodes, L., and N. Shanklin. 1992. *Windows into Literacy: Assessing Learners K-8*. Portsmouth, NH: Heinemann.

Rief, L. 1991. *Seeking Diversity: Language Arts with Adolescents*. Portsmouth, NH: Heinemann.

Rigg, P., and V. Allen, eds. 1989. *When They Don't All Speak English*. Urbana, IL: National Council of Teachers of English.

Rosenblatt, L. 1978. *The Reader, the Text, and the Poem*. Carbondale, IL: Southern Illinois University Press.

Routman, R. 1991. *Invitations: Changing as Teachers and Learners K-12*. Portsmouth, NH: Heinemann.

Short, K., and C. Burke. 1991. *Creating Curriculum: Students and Teachers as a Community of Learners*. Portsmouth, NH: Heinemann.

Short, K., K. Crawford, L. Kahn, S. Kaser, C. Klassen, and P. Sherman. 1992. "Teacher Study Groups: Exploring Literacy Issues Through Collaborative Dialogue." In *Literacy Research, Theory, and Practice: Views from Many Perspectives*, ed. C. Kinzer and D. Leu. Chicago, IL: The National Reading Conference.

Short, K., and K. Pierce. 1990. *Talking About Books: Creating Literate Communities*. Portsmouth, NH: Heinemann.

Smith, F. 1988. *Insult to Intelligence: The Bureaucratic Invasion of Our Classrooms*. Portsmouth, NH: Heinemann.

Steffey, S., and W. Hood, eds. 1994. *If This Is Social Studies, Why Isn't It Boring?* York, ME: Stenhouse.

Stires, S. 1991. *With Promise: Redefining Reading and Writing Needs for "Special" Students*. Portsmouth, NH: Heinemann.

Taba, H. 1966. *Teaching Strategies and Cognitive Functioning in Elementary School Children*. San Francisco: San Francisco State College Press.

Taylor, D. 1983. *Family Literacy: Young Children Learning to Read and Write*. Portsmouth, NH: Heinemann.

———. 1990. *Learning Denied*. Portsmouth, NH: Heinemann.

Teale, W., and E. Sulzby. 1986. "Home Background and Young Children's Literacy Development." In *Emergent Literacy*, ed. W. Teale and E. Sulzby. Norwood, NJ: Ablex.

Tyler, R. 1949. *Basic Principles of Curriculum and Instruction*. Chicago, IL: University of Chicago Press.

Vygotsky, L. 1977. *Thought and Language*. Cambridge, MA: MIT Press.

Weaver, C., ed. 1994. *Success at Last! Helping Students with Attention Deficit (Hyperactivity) Disorders Achieve Their Potential*. Portsmouth, NH: Heinemann.

Weir, R. 1962. *Language in the Crib*. The Hague: Mouton.

Wells, G. 1992. *Constructing Knowledge Together: Classrooms as Centers of Inquiry and Literacy*. Portsmouth, NH: Heinemann.

Whitin, D., H. Mills, and T. O'Keefe. 1990. *Living and Learning Mathematics: Stories and Strategies for Supporting Mathematical Literacy*. Portsmouth, NH: Heinemann.

Whitmore, K., and C. Crowell. 1994. *Inventing a Classroom: Life in a Bilingual, Whole Language Learning Community*. York, ME: Stenhouse.

Wiggins, G. 1989. "The Futility of Trying to Teach Everything of Importance." *Educational Leadership* 47(3): 44–59.

Wilde, S. 1991. *You Kan Red This! Spelling and Punctuation for Whole Language Classrooms*. Portsmouth, NH: Heinemann.

Wortman, R. 1990. "Authenticity in the Writing Events of a Whole Language Kindergarten/First Grade." Ph.D. diss., University of Arizona.

Wortman, R., and M. Matlin Haussler. 1989. "Evaluation in a Classroom Environment Designed for Whole Language." In *The Whole Language Evaluation Book*, ed. K. Goodman, Y. Goodman, and W. Hood. Portsmouth, NH: Heinemann.

Children's Books

Arnold, Tedd. 1992. *The Signmaker's Assistant*. New York: Dial.

Baylor, Byrd. 1986. *Your Own Best Secret Place*. New York: Macmillan.

Bond, Michael. 1960. *A Bear Called Paddington*. New York: Houghton Mifflin.

Bunting, Eve. 1990. *The Wall*. New York: Clarion.

———. 1991. *Fly Away Home*. New York: Clarion.

Burningham, John. 1987. *John Patrick Norman McHennessy: The Boy Who Was Always Late*. New York: Crown.

Cherry, Lynne. 1990. *The Great Kapok Tree*. New York: Harcourt Brace.

Calmenson, Stephanie. 1989. *The Principal's New Clothes*. New York: Scholastic.

Cohen, Miriam. 1980. *First Grade Takes a Test*. New York: Bantam Doubleday Dell.

———. 1987. *When Will I Read?* New York: Bantam Doubleday Dell.

———. 1989. *Will I Have a Friend?* New York: Macmillan.

de Paula, Tomie. 1975. *Strega Nona*. New York: Putnam.

Frasier, Debra. 1991. *On the Day You Were Born*. New York: Harcourt Brace Jovanovich.

Heide, Florence Parry. 1985. *Tales of the Perfect Child*. New York: Bantam Doubleday Dell.

Heine, Henrich. 1986. *Friends*. New York: Macmillan.

Hobermann, Mary Anne. 1978. *A House Is a House for Me*. New York: Viking Penguin.

Houston, Gloria. 1992. *My Great Aunt Arizona*. New York: HarperCollins.

Kellogg, Steven. 1990. *Best Friends*. New York, NY: Doubleday.

Krause, Robert. 1971. *Leo the Late Bloomer*. New York: Simon and Schuster.

Lewin, Ted. 1993. *Amazon Boy*. New York: Macmillan.

Lioni, Leo. 1967. *Frederick*. New York: Simon and Schuster.

Potter, Beatrix. 1986. *Peter Rabbit*. New York: Scholastic.

Rathmann, Peggy. 1991. *Ruby the Copycat*. New York: Scholastic.

Rey, H. A. 1973. *Curious George*. New York: Houghton Mifflin.

Rosen, Michael. 1992. *Home: A Collaboration of Thirty Distinguished Authors and Illustrators of Children's Books to Aid the Homeless*. New York: HarperCollins.

Rylant, Cynthia. 1987. *Henry and Mudge*. New York: Macmillan.

Sendak, Maurice. 1963. *Where the Wild Things Are*. New York: Harper and Row.

Seuss, Dr. 1957. *The Cat in the Hat*. Boston, MA: Houghton Mifflin.

Spier, Peter. 1980. *People*. New York: Doubleday.

Venezia, Mike. 1991. *Paul Klee*. New York: Children's Press.

Viorst, Judith. 1972. *Alexander and the Terrible, Horrible, No Good, Very Bad Day*. New York: Atheneum.

Waber, Bernard. 1973. *The House on East Eighty-Eighth Street*. New York: Houghton Mifflin.

Index